HEROES OF HISTORY

ORVILLE WRIGHT

The Flyer

For my father,
William Douglas Crombie, NZCE
1932–2005
A true lover of all things mechanical.
This one's for you, Dad.
Janet

HEROES OF HISTORY

ORVILLE WRIGHT

The Flyer

JANET & GEOFF BENGE

Emerald Books

P.O. BOX 635, LYNNWOOD, WA 98046

Emerald Books are distributed through YWAM Publishing. For a full list of titles, including other great biographies, visit our website at www.ywampublishing.com or call 1-800-922-2143.

Library of Congress Cataloging-in-Publication Data

Benge, Janet, 1958–
  Orville Wright : the flyer / Janet and Geoff Benge.
     p. cm. — (Heroes of history)
  Includes bibliographical references.
  ISBN-13: 978-1-932096-34-7 (pbk.)
  ISBN-10: 1-932096-34-5 (pbk.)
  1. Wright, Orville, 1871–1948—Juvenile literature. 2. Wright,
Wilbur, 1867–1912—Juvenile literature. 3. Aeronautics—United
States—Biography—Juvenile literature. 4. Wright Flyer
(Airplane)—Juvenile literature. I. Benge, Geoff, 1954– II. Title.
  TL540.W7B46 2006
  629.130092—dc22

                                                          2006006692

Orville Wright: The Flyer

10 09 08 07 06   10 9 8 7 6 5 4 3 2 1

Published by Emerald Books
P.O. Box 635
Lynnwood, Washington 98046

ISBN 1-932096-34-5

Printed in the United States of America.

HEROES OF HISTORY

Biographies

Abraham Lincoln
Benjamin Franklin
Christopher Columbus
Clara Barton
Daniel Boone
Douglas MacArthur
George Washington
George Washington Carver
Harriet Tubman
John Adams
John Smith
Laura Ingalls Wilder
Meriwether Lewis
Orville Wright
Theodore Roosevelt
William Penn

More Heroes of History coming soon!
Unit study curriculum guides are available
for select biographies.

Available at your local bookstore or
through Emerald Books
1 (800) 922-2143

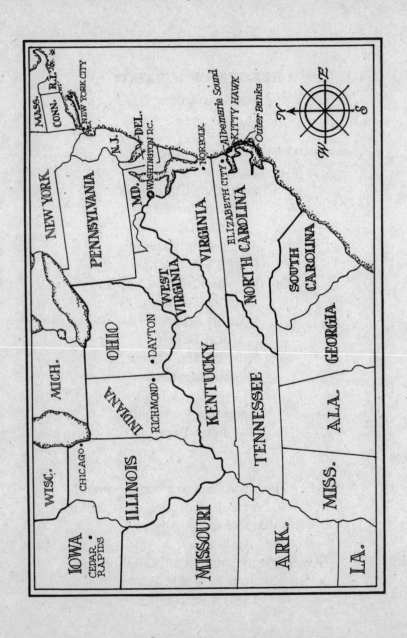

Contents

Chapter 1

Out of Control

Tap. Tap. Tap." *What was that?* It was not the usual sound of the aeroplane's engine. Pilot Orville Wright glanced quickly over his shoulder. Everything looked normal. Still, it was an odd noise, and Orville decided that he should land and check it out. He had wanted everything to go perfectly in this demonstration flight for the U.S. Army, but he knew the dangers of flying too well to dismiss the strange noise, especially with a passenger on board.

Disappointed, Orville signaled to his passenger, Lieutenant Thomas Selfridge, that he was bringing the Flyer in for a landing. Sitting side by side in the revolutionary heavier-than-air flying machine, the two men were traveling about one hundred feet above the ground. Just as Orville was about to dip the nose and guide the Flyer in to land, he heard two loud bangs behind them. Before he had time to think what the bangs could be, the Flyer began to shudder and vibrate.

One of the propeller drive chains must have snapped. The thought flashed through Orville's mind, and Orville instinctively reached over and shut off the engine. But as soon as he shut the engine down, the Flyer veered right toward Arlington Cemetery. Orville quickly pulled on the control levers to regain control of the Flyer. But when he activated the wing-warping control and adjusted the rudder, nothing happened. The Flyer continued veering right.

Orville pulled frantically at the control levers. This time, to his relief, the right wing lifted and the Flyer began to turn in the opposite direction. Orville then activated the wing warping in the opposite direction to bring the Flyer back to level and under control. But as he did so, the nose of the Flyer suddenly dropped. The horizon was gone. Now all Orville could see in front of him was the hard, brown dirt of the parade ground at Fort Myer, Virginia.

"Oh! Oh!" Thomas cried.

Orville gave Thomas a quick glance. His passenger's face was ashen, and his eyes bulged as he stared at the ground rushing toward the Flyer.

Orville made one last desperate attempt to get the nose of the Flyer up and get the craft back under control. He frantically moved the front elevator to its maximum "up" position. *It's beginning to work. It's beginning to work. Yes, the nose is lifting.* But it was too late. *So this is how it ends for the boy from*

Dayton, Ohio, on a dusty parade ground near Washington, D.C., on a September afternoon.

The Flyer slammed nose first into the ground. Orville heard the sound of splintering wood all around him, and dust burst against his face. He felt a searing pain in his left thigh, and then everything went black.

Brothers

Seven-year-old Orville Wright watched in amazement as his father lifted a toy helicopter out of a box and pulled the rubber band wound tightly around it. The twin propellers whirled and pulled the helicopter made of cork, bamboo, and paper into the air, where the toy flew for about ten seconds.

Orville's older brother, Wilbur, ran to grab the helicopter as it reached the grass.

"There you are, boys. I hope you like it," their father, Bishop Milton Wright, said.

Orville grinned. "Of course we do! Wait till we show Mother!"

Milton Wright chuckled. "Yes, knowing your mother, I have no doubt that she'll be just as interested in a flying machine as you two are. Now, don't forget you still have your chores to do before dinner."

"Yes, Father," the two boys answered together.

Bishop Wright walked inside the house while the two brothers took turns pulling the rubber band and twirling the helicopter high into the air. Their sister, four-year-old Katharine, joined them and insisted that she, too, have a turn flying the new toy.

The next day, as Orville sat in his second-grade classroom in Cedar Rapids, Iowa, he could not concentrate on what the teacher was saying. All he could think about was the flying machine his father had brought home the night before and how he could improve it. He wondered whether the helicopter would fly twice as high if it were twice as big. Or would it fly for twice as long? And since it had two propellers, would it go higher if it had four propellers, or six?

The year was 1878, and no answers to such questions existed. Orville reminded himself that only insects, birds, and a few reptiles could fly and they were not telling their secrets to anyone.

The next day Orville found some wood behind the outhouse and started building his own flying machine in the hope of finding answers to some of his questions. Wilbur, who was eleven years old, was a great help in the endeavor. But both boys were disappointed when they could not get their homemade flying machine to lift off the ground under "rubber-band" power. Orville was not used to failure. Just about everything he tried came easily to him. Just a week before he had complained that he was bored using *McGuffey's Second Reader*, and the principal had declared that any second-grade student who could read a passage he or she selected from the book without making an error could go on to the third reader. Since Orville did not want to take any chances, he memorized the entire section he was allocated to read. When it was his turn to read in front of the principal and his teacher, he was so nervous that he held the book upside down. But still he managed to recite the passage perfectly from memory and was allowed to pass on to the next reader.

The two youngest Wright brothers, along with their two older brothers, Reuchlin, who was ten years older than Orville, and Lorin, who was eight years older, played with the toy helicopter until they wore it out. Regrettably, neither Orville nor Wilbur was able to make another one that would fly. The boys did not have the right tools to work with, but that all changed just before Orville's tenth birthday. Soon they would have the equipment to make all kinds of things. It was June 1881, and the Wright family was moving again. The family had moved several times in Orville's lifetime, but this move was one that Orville looked forward to. The family was on its way to Richmond, Indiana, close to Orville's maternal grandparents. Grandpa Koerner was the most fascinating man Orville knew, mostly because he was a carriage maker and had a workshop filled with woodworking tools. And from these tools he could make just about anything he set his mind to. Although Grandpa Koerner was a fastidious German immigrant, Orville hoped that he would trust him and Wilbur to use his tools.

As soon as they arrived in Richmond, Orville and Wilbur begged to go to their grandparents' farm to see the carriage shop, set up in one of the dozen buildings on the property. The two brothers were intrigued with the place. All sorts of metal and wood-working tools were arrayed in the carriage shop, but what really piqued the boys' interest was Grandpa's lathe for turning wood.

Right then and there, Orville and Wilbur decided that they were going to build a lathe of their own. They assembled it in the barn at the back of their house in Richmond. It was a lot of work and challenged their ingenuity, but the boys kept at it. The lathe, like Grandpa's, was powered by a treadle, which Wilbur had decided would run more smoothly if they used a ball-bearing race. He made the balls for the race from clay and set them in a metal ring he found on an old horse harness in the barn. The lathe worked perfectly, and many of the neighborhood children volunteered to work the treadle to turn it. But after a day the clay ball bearings shattered, causing the lathe to shudder and finally grind to a halt.

Nonetheless, living near Grandpa Koerner's workshop inspired Orville and Wilbur to try their hand at inventing all sorts of other things. Orville began building kites, lighter and bigger than the ones his friends had. And soon those friends were begging him to sell his kites to them. Glad to collect the extra pocket money, Orville happily obliged. He and Wilbur decided to use some of the money to stage a production that summer.

Orville had become friends with Gansey Johnson, whose father was a taxidermist. And as Orville surveyed Mr. Johnson's collection of stuffed rare birds and animals, he had come up with an idea. Why not use the stuffed animals to stage a circus? Gansey thought it was a great idea, and the boys were soon busy organizing the event. They enlisted the help of Wilbur to publicize the circus and parade through Richmond. Wilbur, who was now attending high school, wrote a press release for the event. The news release was published under the headline "What Are the Boys Up To?" It promised a "stupendous" show that would feature thousands of stuffed rare birds. Even Davy Crockett and a grizzly bear were to make an appearance in the show.

On the day of the parade, the boys set off through town. They had converted an old wagon for the purpose, and Wilbur had convinced several of his friends to pull the wagon down the main street of Richmond. On the back of the wagon were arranged the stuffed rare birds, "Davy Crockett" (Gansey's four-year-old brother dressed in his father's hunting clothes), and the stuffed grizzly bear. Orville was surprised by the number of people who turned out to see the parade. The crowd followed the parade to the Johnsons' barn, where the boys put on quite a show for the people.

Orville had so much fun living in Richmond that he was disappointed when three years later, in 1884, the Wright family moved once again. This time it was back to Dayton, where they owned a house at 7 Hawthorn Street. In fact, it was the same house Orville had been born in on August 19, 1871, and where he had lived for the first several years of his life. The move to Dayton was not a popular one with the family, but Bishop Wright explained that it was necessary if he was to continue to have a strong influence in the United Brethren in Christ Church. The church was becoming far too liberal for his liking. In particular it was not being strict enough in forbidding church members from joining groups like the Masonic Lodge. Neither Orville nor Wilbur cared much for church doctrine, but the boys had to follow their parents to Dayton.

As they packed their belongings, Mrs. Wright reminded Orville that the family's roots went a long way back in Dayton. In fact, Orville's great-grandmother's sister, Catherine Van Cleve Thompson, had been the first white woman to set foot in Dayton, and her son Benjamin, his grandmother's cousin, had been the town's first postmaster, schoolteacher, librarian, and county clerk.

Before the move to Dayton, Orville's two oldest brothers, Reuchlin and Lorin, set out for Hartsville, Indiana, to attend Hartsville College, which both of their parents had attended.

After having had the run of two farms, the family's long, narrow city lot in Dayton seemed like a prison to Orville. He even got out his measuring tape and learned that their house was only five feet away from the neighbor's house. Still, Orville soon made new friends when he started eighth grade at the local school. And while Orville attended eighth grade, Wilbur, who had graduated from high school in Richmond, decided to take one more year of schooling at Dayton's Central High School to prepare himself to attend Yale Divinity School.

One of Orville's new friends was another eighth grader named Ed Sines. Ed owned a toy printing kit that consisted of a small inkpad and some moveable rubber type. The type could be arranged to form words and then stamped onto a page with ink from the inkpad. Orville was fascinated with the process, and he and Ed spent hours playing with it, stamping out words and building up sentences on paper.

Seeing his son's fascination with the printing set, Milton Wright arranged for Orville to get a small printing press and twenty-five pounds of moveable lead type. The printing press was set up in the Wright house, and Orville and Ed started in on a "printing career." Their first publication was a four-page paper they produced for their eighth-grade class. They called the paper *The Midget*. It was aptly named, since the printing press could print only on sheets of paper the size of postcards.

Both Orville and Wilbur liked to be active, and they played on as many sports teams as they could join. They were always among the top players on their teams. However, one day in March 1886 a game of shinny, a version of ice hockey, changed the course of Wilbur's life. The game was being played on a frozen pond on the outskirts of Dayton. The hockey stick of one of the players flew out of the player's hand and hit Wilbur in the mouth. The blow knocked out several of Wilbur's front teeth. Wilbur fell to the ice as blood erupted from his mouth.

Orville ran to help his brother, as did a doctor who had been watching the boys play. Eventually the bleeding stopped, and Wilbur was escorted home.

Orville watched his brother's agony. For the first few days, Wilbur's jaw was wrapped in a white linen bandage. When the bandage was removed, Wilbur's lips remained swollen and red for days. Wilbur could not eat anything solid and had to be content to nibble on dry toast and take what liquid he could sip through a straw. And because he could not attend school, he withdrew from the college preparation courses he was taking at Central High School. Still, Orville was relieved for his brother when a dentist declared that Wilbur's missing teeth could be replaced with false ones.

While he was sorry about Wilbur's injury, Orville was glad that his brother was at home and able to help out with another tragedy that had befallen the Wright family that winter. Mrs. Wright had been sick for some time and was eventually diagnosed with tuberculosis, a slowly progressing and usually fatal disease of the lungs. Wilbur took care of his mother during the day, sitting by her side and reading to her. But as the days passed, Mrs. Wright began to slowly waste away. It was not an easy time for Orville, and he threw himself into his schoolwork in an effort to take his mind off things at home, hoping all the while that his mother would somehow recover.

Chapter 3

The Safety Bicycle

Wilbur recovered from his injury and had false teeth fitted. Much to Orville's delight, his older brother seemed to emerge from the bout of depression that he had sunk into after the injury. But Orville's delight was tempered by the fact that their mother's condition was growing worse. Since Bishop Wright spent about half of each year traveling on church business, Wilbur assumed the role of organizing the family home and nursing their mother. Orville, for his part, tried to make life as easy as he could for his mother and brother while trying to finish high school.

In his spare time, Orville built a large printing press from various scraps he found around Dayton, including a folding buggy top, a tombstone, and a pile of firewood. When finished, Orville's unique press churned out over a thousand printed sheets of paper an hour. Word of the contraption spread to a large printing firm in Chicago. When visiting Dayton one day, the owner of the company came to see the press at work. As the man closely inspected the press, crawling under it and over it, Orville noted the astonishment that crept across the man's face. Finally he shook his head and patted Orville on the back. "Well, it works," he said, "but I certainly don't see how!"

Orville took the comment as a well-deserved compliment.

The strain of having a dying mother at home, however, proved too much for Orville, who during his final year dropped out of high school. Since the only thing in his life that really interested him was printing, after dropping out of school, Orville began publishing and printing a weekly community paper called the *West Side News*. At eighteen years of age, he was the paper's editor and publisher. The title sounded impressive until people realized that the *West Side News* had a circulation of only four hundred, which Orville hand-delivered on Saturday mornings.

Four months after Orville began publication of the newspaper, Susan Wright died, on July 4, 1889. She was fifty-eight years old. A deep sadness engulfed Orville as he attended his mother's funeral at 2:00 PM on July 6. His mother had been the one who had encouraged his inventiveness. She had always been far handier around the house with tools than his father ever was. In fact, when Orville needed mechanical advice regarding some invention he was trying to build, he always consulted his mother. But now she was gone, and Orville would have to figure out those mechanical problems on his own.

With the death of Mrs. Wright, Wilbur had little to do around the house. He and Orville talked together about the future, and finally they decided that Orville would cease publishing the *West Side News* and together the two brothers would replace it with a more ambitious project, a daily newspaper to be called the *Evening Item.*

The Wright brothers knew that there was no guarantee that this new venture would succeed, as there were over a dozen other daily newspapers vying for readers in the Dayton area. Indeed, it was not a success. Within four months Orville and Wilbur had run out of money to publish and print the newspaper. Instead they turned their attention to printing stationery and various forms for local businesses. This work was repetitious and not nearly as interesting as running a daily newspaper, but it gave Orville and Wilbur enough money to live on.

As Orville worked away in the print shop, he often pondered his future, wondering what might lie in store for him in his life. He knew he had found at least part of the answer to this question when he saw his first "safety bicycle."

Various incarnations of the bicycle had been around for a number of years. As a boy Wilbur had owned an "ordinary" bike. This bike had a large front wheel and small back wheel. To the hub of the front wheel were attached pedals. The rider perched on a sprung seat above the wheel and peddled for all his or her might to keep the contraption upright and moving forward. But these bicycles were bone-jarring and difficult to ride, often sending riders headlong over the handlebars when they hit a rock or a bump in the road.

The safety bicycle was very different. Its wheels were of equal size and were attached to a triangular steel tube frame. The wheels had wire spokes and were fitted with inflatable rubber tires. The back wheel was turned by use of a continuous chain, which was looped around a large cog in the front to which the pedals were attached, and around a smaller cog on the hub of the back wheel. The nature of this ratio allowed the back wheel to turn faster than the rider was pedaling. The bicycle was also fitted with a wide, sprung leather saddle, which, coupled with the wire spokes and inflatable tires, took away most of the bone-jarring aspects of bike riding. It was called a safety bicycle because it was much safer to ride than an ordinary bike, tending to ride over bumps in the road rather than sending the rider hurtling over the handlebars.

The invention of the safety bicycle created quite a stir, and soon men and women were flocking to buy them. A safety bicycle allowed a person to get around quickly without having to rely on streetcars and other forms of public transportation, which were often slow and overcrowded. Bicycles became so popular that one commentator writing in the *Detroit News* noted, "It would not be at all strange if history came to the conclusion that the perfection of the bicycle was the greatest incident in the nineteenth century."

From the first time he laid eyes on one, Orville was fascinated by the new safety bicycle. However, the new invention was not cheap, often costing a quarter of a man's yearly salary. Still, in 1892, Orville could no longer resist the temptation to own a bicycle, and he took every penny of his savings out of the bank and purchased a Columbia, a top-of-the-line bike, for $160.

Ed Sines, Orville's old friend who worked at the print shop with him and Wilbur, also got a bicycle. Together Ed and Orville started a local bike club and joined the YMCA Wheelmen. They also began entering bike races, and much to his delight, Orville won a number of these races. This only served to fuel his enthusiasm for safety bicycles. Finally, Wilbur became interested in bikes and purchased a used one for himself at auction for eighty dollars. Together Orville and Wilbur rode all over Dayton and the surrounding countryside. Orville loved the feel of the wind against his face and the sun on his back as he rode.

Wilbur, Orville, and Ed were not the only ones in Dayton to catch the bicycle craze. People all over the city were busy buying bikes of their own. And with their mechanical know-how, the Wright brothers were soon being asked to make repairs on various bikes. Orville and Wilbur did not mind; it was a nice distraction from the routine of the print shop. But as more and more people sought them out for repairs, the brothers began to wonder whether they might not be able to turn the work into a means to supplement their income from the print shop. "Do you think we can turn this into a paying business?" Orville finally asked his brother one day.

By December 1892 Orville and Wilbur had decided that they could indeed turn it into a paying business, and so they set to work opening a store to sell and repair bicycles. They rented a place in West Dayton, next to a funeral parlor, and spent the winter stocking it with spare parts and accessories, along with a number of high-quality bicycles to sell.

In Ohio cycling was a seasonal activity, with virtually no one venturing out on a bike during the cold winter months. But when spring rolled around, the Wright Cycle Company opened its doors for business.

While Orville and Wilbur busied themselves selling and repairing bikes, Ed ran the print shop with the help of Lorin Wright, Orville and Wilbur's older brother, whom they had hired to work for them. The job suited Lorin well. He lived nearby, and with his wife, Neta, pregnant, he needed the regular income.

Business at the Wright Cycle Company was brisk throughout its first season of operation. Orville and Wilbur filled their days mending flat tires, replacing broken spokes, and straightening bent front forks. They also sold a number of bikes, sometimes by arranging a time payment plan for a customer or by taking in an old bike as a trade-in on the new one. They also rented bikes by the hour and by the day.

To help promote their business, Orville and Wilbur began publishing a weekly newsletter called

Snap-Shots of Current Events for the bicycle enthusiasts of Dayton. The newsletter contained articles
about bicycling, humorous anecdotes and jokes,
and of course, advertising for the Wright Cycle
Company. The Wright brothers also sold advertising in the newsletter to local merchants.

When it opened for business, the Wright Cycle
Company was one of only a few cycle shops in
Dayton. But by 1895 the town had fourteen bicycle
businesses, three of which were located within two
blocks of Orville and Wilbur's shop. As a result of
the competition, prices got lower and lower, until
Orville and Wilbur felt that they could lower them
no more and still make a profit. The brothers began
to look for new ways to broaden their company and
bring in new customers. Because they had been
selling and repairing bikes for over two years now,
Orville and Wilbur were familiar with the strengths
and weaknesses of the various models they sold.
Drawing on this knowledge, they decided to begin
designing and building their own bicycles.

Twenty-four-year-old Orville and twenty-eight-
year-old Wilbur set to work. First they had to set up
a machine shop in the back of their store where they
could manufacture the new bikes. They installed a
turret lathe, a drill press, and a machine for cutting
steel tubing. Once the machines were in place,
Orville and Wilbur needed to provide a means to
drive them. They did this by installing a rotating
shaft along the wall, from which belts were connected to the machines. Their next challenge was
an engine to spin the shaft. The brothers decided to
build their own single-cylinder internal-combustion

engine. The engine was designed to run on coal gas that was piped to the bicycle store by city pipeline. As they built the engine, Orville focused on the valve lifters and the timing of the ignition spark, while Wilbur took care of the governor, which kept the engine running smoothly at a set speed, and devised a method to keep the motor cool while it was running. Before long the single-cylinder engine was puttering away at the back of the cycle store, spinning the shaft and driving the machines, just as it was supposed to.

Besides installing the machines and building an engine to power them, the two brothers had to devise some equipment that would allow them to electric arc weld together the steel tube frames of the new bikes. When everything was finally installed and running, Orville and Wilbur set to work building the new bicycles they had designed. In April 1896 they advertised their new bikes in *Snap-Shots of Current Events:*

> The Wright Special will contain nothing but high grade materials throughout, although we shall put it on the market at the exceedingly low price of $60. It will have large tubing, high frame, tool steel bearings, needle wire spokes, narrow tread and every feature of an up-to-date bicycle. Its weight will be 22 pounds. We are very certain that no wheel on the market will run easier or wear longer than this one, and we will guarantee it in the most unqualified manner.

Orville and Wilbur also manufactured the Van Cleve line of bicycles and then, later, the less expensive St. Clair line. Soon orders for the new bikes started rolling in, and Orville and Wilbur were kept busier than ever producing them.

Katharine, who was now attending Oberlin College, returned home for the summer, where she took care of duties around the house. In late August, just as she was getting ready to return to college for her junior year, Orville came home not felling well. Katharine tucked him into bed to recuperate. But instead of feeling better, Orville began to feel worse. His temperature was climbing rapidly, and he was beginning to get feverish. There was no denying the obvious. Orville had somehow contracted typhoid fever. While the disease was often fatal, Orville felt so feverish and wretched he hardly cared whether he lived or died. He became delirious and began to float in and out of consciousness.

All Orville could remember of the next six weeks was occasionally opening his eyes to see Wilbur or Katharine sitting at his bedside or being aware of someone force-feeding him milk or beef broth.

Finally Orville's fever broke, and on October 8, 1896, Orville sat up in bed for the first time in six weeks and ate a bowl of tapioca. Wilbur and Katharine looked relieved to see him fully conscious again. The following morning, Katharine, who was already a month late for classes, set off for Oberlin College while Wilbur nursed his brother back to full health.

Over the next few days, Wilbur filled his brother in on some of the things he had read while sitting at Orville's bedside. For one thing, in early August the German aviation pioneer Otto Lilienthal had been killed when his glider stalled in midair and crashed to the ground. "You remember him, don't you?" Wilbur asked, "He was the German aviator we read about in *McClure's* magazine two years ago—the man who had studied birds in flight and then built gliders that mimicked the shape of their wings."

Orville nodded.

Wilbur went on. "And you remember that before you got sick, Langley finally got one of his aerodromes to fly. Well, now Octave Chanute and his team have successfully flown a glider based on one of Lilienthal's designs."

Again Orville nodded.

Samuel Pierpont Langley was the secretary of the Smithsonian Institution in Washington. He had undertaken a study of aeronautics to see whether it was indeed scientifically possible to construct a heavier-than-air flying machine. His conclusion was that it was possible and that "mechanical flight is possible with the engines we now possess." But after Langley released his results in 1891, the scientific community had remained skeptical of his findings. Some had even questioned the method by which he had undertaken his study.

Fearing that his reputation as a scientist was under attack, Langley decided to build and fly a model of such a heavier-than-air craft. He named his craft an aerodrome. He built one model aerodrome after another, which were then launched from a catapult mounted atop a houseboat on the

Potomac River. Each of his models, however, crashed into the river immediately after launch. Then, on the afternoon of May 6, 1896, one of his models did not crash. Instead, Aerodrome No. 5 began to climb and circle in the sky around the houseboat. Powered by a miniature steam engine that drove two rear-facing propellers, it looked something like a dragonfly with a fourteen-foot wingspan. It flew for ninety seconds before its head of steam was exhausted and it sank slowly down and settled on the surface of the river. Langley's men fished it out, dried it off, and, after they had produced another head of steam, flew the craft again. Finally, by popular demonstration, Samuel Pierpont Langley had proved his scientific findings had been right all along.

Octave Chanute was a French immigrant who had become one of America's most celebrated civil engineers. On a trip back to France with his family, Chanute had become interested in the quest to build a flying machine. Back in the United States, he held several symposia to discuss and popularize the idea. He also gathered around him a number of aviation pioneers and innovators, and together they began building and testing a number of gliders. Like Langley, Chanute and his men were confronted with one failure after another until August 29, 1896, when, using a modified version of one of Lilienthal's glider designs, they were able to glide for over 150 feet. After repeated flights, they stretched that distance to 359 feet and managed to stay aloft for fourteen seconds.

As Orville listened to Wilbur relay to him news of Chanute's success, little did he know that in the years ahead, his and Wilbur's paths and that of Octave Chanute would be closely intertwined.

After making a full recovery, Orville went back to work at the bicycle shop, building new bikes to sell in the spring. But the work was routine. The real challenge had been to set up and equip the machine shop and design and build the first bikes. Now that the challenge was gone, Orville began to wonder what new challenge might lie ahead for him.

On June 22, 1898, Katharine Wright graduated from Oberlin College and returned home for good. She took a job as a Latin teacher at the local high school and set about keeping house for her father and two brothers. Orville, for one, was glad to have his younger sister home. He had always liked her company, and even though he and Wilbur were meticulously clean and tidy, there was something about a woman's touch about the house.

As the months rolled by, Orville began to wonder whether the new challenge he sought might have something to do with aviation. He and Wilbur began to talk about how man might fly and how a heavier-than-air craft, large enough to carry a man, might be built. Mostly it was idle chatter, until early in 1899, when Orville and Wilbur read a book on ornithology. As a result of reading the book, Wilbur became inspired to observe birds in flight, paying close attention to the shape of their wings and the movements of their bodies as they flew. To do this he rode his bicycle out to a place called the Pinnacles, a rocky outcrop that jutted above the Miami River. At the end of the day, Wilbur would explain to Orville how, sitting of the edge of the outcrop, he had watched hawks and buzzards circling above. He talked about how the birds barely flapped their wings to stay aloft but rather relied on making small adjustments to the shape of their wings or on moving their body slightly from side to side. He explained that as small as these motions were, they seemed to keep the birds gliding for hours. He also observed that most often a bird made not a single but a number of small gestures together to adjust its position in the air.

Orville listened to all that Wilbur told him, and in the evenings the brothers sat around the fire and talked about what these observations might mean for the design and construction of an airplane.

Chapter 4

Enthusiasts
but Not Cranks

L isten to this!" Wilbur said as Orville walked in the
 door of the Wright home at 7 Hawthorn Street.
As usual their father, Milton, was away on church
business. The aroma of the roast beef Katharine
was preparing for dinner filled the house and made
Orville's mouth water. He hung up his hat and coat
and sat down in his favorite chair by the fireplace.

Wilbur cleared his throat and continued. "This
is a quote from Louis Mouillard. I just found it in
an old copy of the Smithsonian Institution's annual
report that I got from the library. 'If there be a dom-
ineering, tyrant thought, it is the conception that
the problem of flight may be solved by man. When
once this idea has invaded the brain it possesses it
exclusively. It is then a haunting thought, a walk-
ing nightmare, impossible to cast off.'"

Orville laughed, recognizing the name of the French aviation pioneer. "We have certainly spent a lot of time pondering the problem of flight, haven't we, Will?"

Wilbur nodded. "I hope we don't get obsessed with it. Still, I was wondering whether, now that we have sold the printing business, we should get more serious about this whole flying endeavor. What do you think?"

The two brothers discussed the idea, and eventually Wilbur decided that he should write to the Smithsonian Institution and ask what kinds of new information they had regarding the possibility of flight.

Two days later, on May 30, 1899, Wilbur presented a draft of the letter to Orville to peruse. The letter was neatly written on Wright Cycle Company letterhead and read,

The Smithsonian Institution
Washington

Dear Sirs:

I have been interested in the problem of mechanical and human flight ever since as a boy I constructed a number of bats of various sizes after the style of Cayley's and Penaud's machines. My observations since have only convinced me more firmly that human flight is feasible and practicable. It is only a question of knowledge and skill just as in all acrobatic feats. Birds are the most perfectly trained gymnasts in the world and are specially well fitted for their work, and it may be that man will never equal them, but no one who has watched a bird chasing an insect or another bird can doubt that feats are performed which require three or four times the effort required by ordinary flight. I believe that simple flight at least is possible to man and that the experiments and investigations of a large number of independent workers will result in the accumulation of information and knowledge and skill which will finally lead to accomplished flight.

The works on this subject to which I have had access are Marey's and Jamieson's books published by Appleton's and various magazine and cyclopedia articles. I am about to begin a systematic study of the subject in preparation for practical work to which I expect to devote what time I can spare from my regular business. I wish to obtain such papers as the Smithsonian Institution has published on the subject, and if possible a list of other works in print in the English language. I am an enthusiast, but not a crank in the sense that I have some pet theories as to the proper construction of a flying machine. I wish to avail myself of all that is already known and then if possible add my mite to help on the future worker who will attain final success. I do not know the terms on which you send out your publications but if you will inform me of the cost I will remit the price.

Orville liked what he read, and after Wilbur mailed the letter off, the two brothers waited eagerly for a reply.

Within a month a thick envelope arrived at the door of the Wright house in Dayton. The envelope contained four pamphlets on the latest information regarding flying, including the article by Mouillard. It also contained a price list of other books on the subject of flight. The brothers ordered the books at once and were soon engulfed in reading Octave Chanute's five-year-old article, *Progress in Flying Machines,* and Samuel Pierpoint Langley's *Experiments in Aerodynamics.*

Both Orville and Wilbur were surprised by how few facts these books actually contained. It seemed that people had lots of opinions regarding flight, based on scarce and shaky factual information. Wilbur joked to his brother that it was not surprising that the flying machines that these people built to test their theories did just about everything but fly!

As Orville and Wilbur worked side by side in the bicycle shop, they discussed what they had read, concluding that to solve the problem of human flight, four different areas had to be examined.

The first area had to do with the engine. Inventors were trying to use steam engines to power their flying machines, as Langley had on his aerodrome model. But steam engines were much too heavy for the purpose. Orville and Wilbur concluded that an internal combustion engine would be better for the purpose. The only problem was that no one had yet built one suitable for the job.

The second area that needed careful study was the shape of the wings. Both Chanute and Lilienthal had crafted wings that seemed to work well enough for a flying machine to glide through the air. But further study was still needed in this area.

The third category related to the structure of the flying machine. Again, Chanute led the way here. As a civil engineer, he had used lightweight materials to build machines that, in theory, should be able to stay airborne.

As far as Wilbur and Orville were concerned, the fourth area posed the biggest challenge. If they could get a flying machine up into the air and propel it forward with a lightweight engine, how were they going to steer it in the air and bring the craft in for a soft landing? To date no one seemed to have studied this problem much, yet a flying machine was almost useless if it could not be controlled once in the air.

Wilbur told Orville that he believed that it was this fourth area that they needed to focus on. Wilbur explained that a flying machine would have three ranges of motion that would need to be controlled once it was in the air. The first range of motion was *pitch*. This was defined as the movement of the nose of the craft up and down around an imaginary axis that ran through the wings. The second was *roll*. This was the ability of the craft to move from side to side along an axis that ran the length of the flying machine. The third range of motion was *yaw*, the movement to the nose of the craft from side to side around an axis that ran through the machine from top to bottom. In this way a flying machine would balance in the air at the point where these three axes crossed.

Wilbur explained that from his observations so far, he had ascertained that birds maintained their balance in the air by making small adjustments in the shape of their wings and in slight shifts in their bodies. "So if a bird wants to turn or adjust its position in the air, it moves the tips of its wings, one tip up and one tip down. This change of shape causes one wing to rise and the other to drop, and the bird moves in a banking turn in the direction of the wing that is dipped."

"It's a bit like riding a bike," Orville interjected.

"Exactly," said Wilbur. "If you want to make a turn on a bike, you use a series of small movements that alter the bike's balance. So you nudge the handlebars gently in the direction you want to go, but at the same time you shift your body weight in that direction, and the bike arcs around in a sloping turn. And when you have achieved the change in direction, you straighten the handlebars and shift your weight back to the center, and the bike becomes upright again and heads in a straight line. I think we are going to find that controlling a flying machine in the air is going to be a lot like controlling a bicycle."

Over the next several weeks, Orville and Wilbur talked about a mechanism that might work to change the plane of the wings so that the flying machine could turn. They decided that a good approach would be to have wing extensions separate from the wings. These extensions could then be angled, one up and one down with the use of metal shafts and gears from the center of the airplane. But the men soon realized that this solution would be altogether too heavy, and they began to look for a new solution.

It was the third week of July 1899, and Orville had taken the day off from the cycle shop to help Katharine with some errands. It had been a stiflingly hot day, and late in the afternoon, Orville sat on the veranda enjoying a gentle breeze that had blown in. Wilbur came bounding up to the house from the cycle shop. "I've found the answer," he blurted out.

Orville looked a little puzzled. "What answer?"

"To the wing control problem," Wilbur said, sitting down beside his brother, an empty inner-tube box in his hand. "And this is the answer," he said, holding up the box.

Again Orville looked confused.

Wilbur went on. "A customer came in wanting to buy a new inner tube for his bike. I pulled one off the shelf and slid it out of its box. As I talked to the customer, I fiddled with the box, twisting one end one way and the other end the other way. And when I looked down and saw what I was doing, it hit me. Look..." Wilbur held up the empty tube box, which was about two inches square and ten inches long, and flexed it the way he had in the bicycle shop.

Immediately Orville's face lit up. As Wilbur twisted the box, the fingers of his left hand caused the box to drop a little as the top side slid forward. Meanwhile Wilbur's right fingers caused the front edge of the other end to drop slightly as the top of the box slid backward. Orville saw what his brother had seen. If you thought of the top and bottom sides of the box as wings, the slight movement on the left side down and forward would expose more of the undersurface of the wing, while the movement at the other end of the wing down and back would expose more of the top side of the wing surface. This warping movement of the wings would achieve the same goal as the wing extenders they had envisaged, causing the aircraft to bank and turn toward the right. And if you wanted to go in the other direction, all you would have to do would be to warp the wings the opposite way. It was an ingenious solution, Orville had to admit, and all from an empty inner tube box.

"Do you think you can make it work?" Orville asked.

Wilbur nodded. "Yes, I think I can," he replied.

Over the next several days, Orville kept watch as Wilbur made sketch after sketch of the idea until he was satisfied with the design. What Wilbur came up with was a pair of wings held together by vertical struts attached by wire loops that would allow the planes of the upper and lower wings to warp forward or backward. The wings were strengthened in a way that would allow them to warp when a control rod pulled a cord, which in turn twisted or warped the wings.

"Now it's time to test the design," Wilbur announced.

Orville kept the cycle store running while Wilbur set to work. Each night Orville would inspect his

brother's progress. Using spilt bamboo, Wilbur constructed a kite, not just any kite but an exact
replica of the warping wings he had designed. Each
wing was about five feet wide, and the top one was
mounted thirteen inches above the bottom. A fixed
elevator was attached at the center back of the kite
to help with stability. Cords were attached to the
top and bottom of the outside wing strut on each
side of the wing, and the ends of the cord were
attached to two control sticks. Wilbur explained that
if the control sticks were both pivoted forward, this
would allow the top wing to slide back and cause
the kite to climb. If they were pivoted the other way,
the wing would move forward, changing the center
of balance, and the nose of the kite would drop.
And if one stick was pivoted one way and the other
stick the other way, the wing should warp and
cause the kite to bank into a turn.

On July 24 Wilbur was putting the final touches
to his kite when Orville left to go on a camping trip
with Katharine and several of her friends. Orville, of
course, would have loved to have stayed behind
and help Wilbur fly the kite, but he had promised
Katharine that he would accompany her and her
friends on the trip long before Wilbur came up with
his insights into warping the wings. Two weeks
later, on August 6, 1899, an excited Wilbur came
out to visit the campsite. An equally excited Orville
ran to greet him.

"It worked perfectly," Wilbur beamed.

Orville was eager to hear all the details. After
Wilbur had greeted everyone at camp, Orville led

him down alongside the river where they could talk. Wilbur told his brother the whole story.

"When the kite was finally finished and I had determined that its controls would work as they were supposed to, I went out to a field near Bonebrake Seminary in West Dayton. Several local boys accompanied me. When a breeze came up, they launched the kite, and it took to the air while I controlled it."

Orville watched his thirty-two-year-old brother's face shine like a boy's as Wilbur explained how well the kite had flown. The wing-warping approach had worked perfectly, and when Wilbur had pivoted the control sticks in opposite directions, one wing dropped and the other rose as the kite banked into a turn.

"All in all, I would call the experiment a success," Wilbur declared, "but it's only the beginning. We still have a lot of experimenting to do. Nonetheless, I think we are on the right road to one day building a powered flying machine that can easily be controlled while it keeps a man aloft."

"I hope you are right, Will," Orville said. "I guess only time will tell."

Wilbur nodded. "Yes, we might not have much else, but we do have time."

Chapter 5

In Search of a Windy Location

When Orville arrived home from the camping trip, he found Wilbur hard at work designing the next kite to test. He explained to Orville that this next kite would be big enough to hold the weight of a man while flying.

"But before I can design it," Wilbur explained, "I need to know how big the wings have to be."

Orville nodded.

"I've found an equation in Lilienthal's writings that should give me the answer. I just need to put in the right values and coefficients and solve the equation, and I should have my answer."

Several days later an excited Wilbur explained to Orville that he had solved the equation and that the wings of the new glider would need to have a surface area of about two hundred square feet. A craft with wings of that size would hold 190 pounds aloft in a steady wind of approximately fifteen miles per hour. One hundred ninety pounds, he explained, was the weight of the glider, 50 pounds, plus his body weight, 140 pounds.

Wilbur had calculated that to get two hundred square feet of wing surface, the wings would have to be eighteen feet long from tip to tip and five feet wide from leading edge to trailing edge. The Wright brothers then discussed the proper shape of the wings. The wings had to provide *lift* so that the glider would stay in the air. At the same time, the wings had to be designed in such a way so as to compensate for *drag*, which was defined as the action of friction and other forces that slowed the forward motion of the wing through the air. When the rear edge of a plank of wood lying flat in a wind is tilted down, the wind catches the underside of the plank, forcing it up (lift) and back (drag). If the plank is turned sideways to the wind, it loses all lift, and drag takes over as the force of the wind pushes it backward. For Wilbur the challenge was to produce a wing that provided maximum lift with as little drag as possible.

"Otto Lilienthal used an arc-shaped wing with a high degree of curvature," Wilbur explained. "I followed his design in the small glider that I flew, but I have my doubts about that design for a larger wing. I think it might create too much drag."

"So how do you propose to modify the design?" Orville asked.

"I'm thinking about reducing the amount of curvature in the wing and moving the apex of the curve forward, close to the leading edge, and gently sloping it out over the rest of the wing. That should greatly reduce the drag and improve the lift of the wings."

And that is what Wilbur did. Soon he was showing Orville the plans he had come up with for the new glider. Like the smaller glider he had flown, this craft had a pair of wings held together by vertical struts attached in such a way as to allow the wings to warp. The wings were strengthened by the use of wire that crisscrossed between the struts. The elevator, or rudder, as Wilbur called it, that had been attached to the rear of the smaller glider was now mounted in the front, where the pilot, using levers and rods, could adjust its angle. The pilot lay facedown in a cutaway section in the center of the bottom wing, and a T-shaped pedal attached to the wing-warping mechanism allowed the pilot to control the wing-warping while in flight.

Orville was very impressed with his brother's plans. Wilbur had obviously put a lot of thought and research into them, and they showed that he had a good grasp on the problem of flight.

Once the plans were finished, Wilbur and Orville turned their attention back to the business of the cycle shop. By now it was fall and time to start building new bicycles to sell the following spring and summer.

As they built the new bikes, the brothers talked about the best place to fly their new glider once it was constructed. They decided that trying to fly it around Dayton was impractical. The wind in that part of Ohio was neither strong enough nor constant enough to fly the glider.

"What about Chicago?" Orville asked as he put the front wheel on the new Van Cleve bicycle he was building. "It's supposed to be the windiest city in the country, and it is reasonably close by."

Wilbur continued welding a new bike frame for a few minutes before answering. "Chicago is certainly windy enough, but I worry about all those reporters. When Chanute was testing his glider in the dunes south of the city, reporters got wind of what he was up to and flocked to the site. I don't want to have to deal with that. I prefer to test the glider somewhere more secluded."

By May 1900 the Wright brothers still had not settled on a suitable place to fly their glider.

"I'm going to write to Chanute and seek his advice on a location to fly the kite," Wilbur told Orville.

On May 13 Wilbur showed Orville the letter he had written. Orville read his brother's words with interest.

For some years I have been afflicted with the belief that flight is possible to man. My disease has increased in severity and I feel that it will soon cost me an increased amount of money if not my life. I have been trying to arrange my affairs in such a way that I can devote my entire time for a few months to experiment in this field.

The letter went on for several pages, laying out just how Wilbur intended to conduct his experiments.

> I shall in a suitable locality erect a light tower of about one hundred and fifty feet high.... The wind will blow the machine out from the base of the tower and the weight will be sustained partly by the upward pull of the rope and partly by the lift of the wind.

Wilbur further explained that by using this approach, he hoped to be able to stay in the air on the glider for several hours at a time. In so doing, he said, he hoped to "escape accident long enough to acquire skill sufficient to prevent accident." He then got to the crux of his letter by asking Chanute for "such suggestions as your great knowledge and experience might enable you to give." Wilbur added that he would be "particularly thankful for advice as to a suitable locality where [he] could depend on winds of about fifteen miles per hour without rain or too inclement weather."

"That's a good letter, Will," Orville said after he had read it. "Let's hope Mr. Chanute has some good suggestions."

Several days after sending off the letter, Wilbur received a reply from Octave Chanute. After reading it, he handed it over to Orville to read. The letter was warm and detailed. Chanute said that he was "quite in sympathy with your proposal to experiment." He went on to say, "I have preferred preliminary learning on a sand hill." As regards to locations with steady winds, he said that steady winds suitable for gliding could be found at Pine Island, Florida, and San Diego, California. However, there were no sand hills at either location. "Perhaps," he suggested, "even better locations can be found on the Atlantic coast of South Carolina or Georgia." Before ending his letter, Chanute sounded a warning about the danger of testing the glider while tethered to a tower, as the tethering ropes were both an extra complication and a safety hazard. "I shall be pleased to correspond with you further," he invited in closing.

"Mr. Chanute certainly gives a lot of information," Orville declared after reading the letter. "But he doesn't exactly answer the question of where to test the glider."

"No, he doesn't," Wilbur replied. "I think I will write to the U.S. Weather Bureau in Washington and request information on the prevailing wind conditions in various parts of the country."

Two weeks later a letter arrived from the Weather Bureau in response to Wilbur's request. The information contained the *Monthly Weather Review* for the months of August and September 1899. These publications contained a table of the hourly wind velocities that had been recorded at the 120 Weather Bureau stations located around the United States. The table confirmed that Chicago, which Wilbur had already dismissed as a suitable location, was indeed the windiest city in the country. Neither were the next four windiest locations suitable for flying a glider, either because they were not isolated or because they did not have the necessary sandy area nearby.

But the sixth location on the list, a place called Kitty Hawk, North Carolina, had an average wind speed during September of 13.4 miles per hour. Neither brother had ever heard of the place, but when they looked it up on a map, they discovered that it was located on the Outer Banks of North Carolina, just north of Cape Hatteras. The Outer Banks was a long string of barrier islands that ran down the Atlantic coasts of North and South Carolina and Georgia. It looked like a promising site at which to test the glider, and so Wilbur and Orville decided to investigate the place.

Wilbur quickly drafted a letter to Joseph Dosher, who manned the Weather Bureau station there. Dosher wrote back, saying, "I will say the beach here is about one mile wide, clear of trees or high hills, and extends for nearly sixty miles same condition."

Several days later another letter arrived from Kitty Hawk, North Carolina. This letter was from William Tate, a Currituck County commissioner, notary public, and former postmaster at Kitty Hawk. The letter read:

Mr. J. J. Dosher of the Weather Bureau has asked me to answer your letter to him, relative to the fitness of Kitty Hawk as a place to practice or experiment with a flying machine, etc.

In answering I would say that you would find here nearly any type of ground you could wish; you could, for instance, get a stretch of sandy land one mile by five with a bare hill in center 80 feet high, not a tree or bush anywhere to break the evenness of the wind current. This in my opinion would be a fine place; our winds are always steady, generally from 10 to 20 miles velocity per hour.

You can reach here from Elizabeth City, N.C. (35 miles from here) by boat directly from Manteo (12 miles from here by mail boat) every Mon., Wed., & Friday. We have Telegraph communications & daily mails. Climate healthy, you could find good place to pitch tents & get board in private family provided there were not too many in your party; would advise you to come any time from September 15 to October 15. Don't wait until November. The autumn generally gets a little rough by November.

If you decide to try your machine here & come I will take pleasure in doing all I can for your convenience & success & pleasure, & I assure you you will find a hospitable people when you come among us.

William Tate's letter settled the issue. Orville and Wilbur would test their new glider at Kitty Hawk, North Carolina. Together the brothers came up with a plan. Wilbur would travel to Kitty Hawk alone in early September, set up camp there, and assemble the glider. As soon as the cycle business tailed off later that month, Orville would join Wilbur. In the meantime the brothers were kept busy with their bicycle business. It was the height of the cycling season, and a steady flow of customers came into the store wanting to buy bikes or have their bikes repaired. It was not until late July, as business began to slow a little, that Wilbur was able to start making the parts for the new glider.

As Orville kept up with the bicycle business, he watched his brother cut lengths of ash wood and bend them, using steam to form the ribs that would give the wings their curved shape. Wilbur then cut and shaped another fifty or so wooden pieces that would form the struts and other parts of the glider. He bought or made the metal fittings that were needed to hold the glider together, and he purchased several spools of 15-gauge spring steel wire that would be used to truss, or strengthen, the wings. Wilbur also purchased yards of sateen fabric and, using Katharine's sewing machine, sewed together the fabric panels that would cover the wings.

One part of the new glider, however, Wilbur could not prepare: the eighteen foot-long spruce wing spars that would run the length of the wings and to which the ribs would be fastened. Wilbur visited all of the lumberyards in Dayton, but not one of them had spruce planks that long that could be cut down for the spars. As a result, Wilbur explained to Orville that he would purchase the spruce spars when he got to Norfolk, Virginia.

At six-thirty in the evening on Thursday, September 6, 1900, Orville and Katharine stood on the station platform at Union Station in Dayton, saying good-bye to Wilbur. Stowed aboard the train in several large trunks were all the parts for the glider Wilbur had made. Finally the guard blew his whistle, and Wilbur jumped aboard the train. "I'll write and let you know how I get on as soon as I arrive," Wilbur called as the train pulled away from the station.

"And I will see you soon in Kitty Hawk," Orville called back.

Orville kept busy at the bicycle shop while he eagerly awaited a letter from Wilbur. Finally, a little over a week after Wilbur had set out, a letter arrived. Orville tore it open and read. The letter began by saying that at six o'clock the night after setting out, Wilbur had made it to Old Point Comfort, where he had caught a ferry across Hampton Roads to Norfolk, Virginia. The following day, in stifling heat, he had gone in search of the spruce spars he needed for the wings. Unfortunately he had been unable to find any, and in the end he had had to settle for sixteen-and-a-half-foot-long white pine spars. He explained to Orville that the shorter spars meant that the wings would have a surface area of only about 177 square feet. To compensate for this smaller wing area, they would have to fly the glider in a stronger wind.

From Norfolk Wilbur had traveled on by train to Elizabeth City, North Carolina. To his surprise, no one there seemed to know much about Kitty Hawk. It took Wilbur three days before he finally met a local captain named Israel Perry, who agreed to take him to Kitty Hawk in his fishing schooner. When he finally boarded the schooner, Wilbur was surprised at the dilapidated condition of the ship. The vessel was so dirty and vermin-invested that Wilbur decided to stay on deck during the trip rather than venture inside.

The voyage had started out well as the schooner sailed down the Pasquotank River from Elizabeth City. But when it reached Albemarle Sound and headed east toward the Outer Banks, the ship ran into a fierce storm. The wind battered the schooner, and the waves broke over her bow, causing Wilbur and Perry's son to keep busy bailing water from the vessel. Then the wind blew loose first the foresail and then the mainsail. Wilbur and Perry's son managed to haul the sails in, but the schooner was in trouble. Thankfully Perry was a better sailor than his vessel belied, and he managed to skillfully turn the boat in treacherous seas. Under the power of nothing but a jib, he also managed to get the schooner to refuge in the channel of the North River, where the boat and its three occupants spent a long night. The following morning the storm had abated, and the Perrys and Wilbur set to work repairing the torn sails. By midafternoon they were again under way, and they finally reached Kitty Hawk that evening. Wilbur spent another night sleeping on the deck of the schooner. The following morning he unloaded his trunks and baggage and went in search of William Tate.

Orville put down the letter for a moment, a little shocked that so much could go wrong in such a short amount of time. He certainly hoped that his upcoming trip to Kitty Hawk would not be as eventful as his brother's had been.

Wilbur was a long letter writer, and this letter still had several pages to go. Orville read on. Wilbur reported that Kitty Hawk was indeed a desolate and isolated place but also a very beautiful place. William Tate and his wife, Addie, were a warm and hospitable couple. When Addie learned that Wilbur had eaten nothing but the small jar of fruit jelly Katharine had packed in his bag throughout his two days and nights on the schooner, she immediately fixed him a meal of ham and eggs. The Tates had a spare room in their roughhewn two-story home, and they insisted that Wilbur stay with them while he assembled his glider.

Wilbur had set up a canvas lean-to in the Tates' front yard and began assembling the glider. His effort was attracting a ragtag parade of locals, fishermen, and Coast Guard lifesavers from the nearby lifesaving station who came by each day to see his progress. Addie was going to loan Wilbur her sewing machine so that he could alter the size of the sateen panels that would cover the wings. Wilbur anticipated that assembly of the glider would take at least a couple of more weeks. Then they would be ready to start flying it.

After reading his brother's letter, Orville looked forward to getting to Kitty Hawk. He felt he already knew the place.

Chapter 6

Kitty Hawk

On September 24, 1900, Orville boarded a train bound for North Carolina. He leaned out the window and gave a final wave to Katharine as the train chugged away from the station. Soon he was sitting alone, being whisked through the Ohio countryside. Recently harvested fields stretched out to the horizon on either side of the train. Orville thought about everything packed away in his father's old trunk, safely stowed in the luggage car. The trunk held two folding cots, four woolen blankets, the very latest acetylene bicycle lamp, the tea, coffee, and sugar that Wilbur had requested, and several jars of Katharine's homemade blackberry jam. Orville hoped that he had brought e̶̶ ̶̶ ̶̶ ̶ith him, as Wilbur had made it sound as̶ ̶ thing was available for sale at Ki̶ planned to stock up on tinned goods and other food items as well once he reached Elizabeth City.

Orville tried not to concern himself about the bicycle shop. He had left the shop in the hands of a young friend named Harry Dillon. Harry had strict instructions to consult with Katharine or Lorin if any unusual problems arose. As for the normal repair work, Cordy Ruse had agreed to do this on a piece-by-piece arrangement. Orville had complete confidence in Cordy, who had constructed Dayton's first horseless carriage and was very familiar with the workings of a bicycle.

The train chugged on through the afternoon and into the night. By the following morning, Orville could feel his excitement growing. Before this he had never ventured farther afield from Dayton than Chicago and he had never seen the ocean. But before this day was over, that was going to change, and he tried to imagine what such a great expanse of salt water would look like.

Finally, at midmorning, the trained pulled into Elizabeth City, North Carolina. Orville disembarked and retrieved his trunk and other items from the baggage car. Elizabeth City sat at the edge of the Pasquotank River, several miles above where it joined Albemarle Sound, a large inlet that led to the Atlantic Ocean. However, between the mouth of the sound and the open ocean lay the Outer Banks, a series of long, thin barrier islands, many of them joining at low tide, that stretched all the way down the coast of North Carolina. Kitty Hawk sat on the barrier island irectly opposite the mouth of Albemarle Sound.

It had taken Wilbur three days to find someone to take him to Kitty Hawk by boat, but Orville had more luck than his brother had had. Soon after arriving at Elizabeth City, he was able to find a sailboat that would take him and his trunk to Kitty Hawk. As they set out down the Pasquotank River, Orville thought of Wilbur's harrowing experience on this same stretch of water a little over two weeks before. He was relieved to discover that the wind was light when the boat finally turned into Albemarle Sound and began heading east.

From the moment he laid eyes on the sound, Orville knew that he was going to enjoy being by the ocean. The sea was even more amazing than he had imagined. He could feel the taste of salt on his tongue as the wind whipped a fine mist of salty spray from the crest of the waves. And all about the sound was dotted with fishing boats coming and going or bobbing gently at anchor along the shoreline.

To his surprise, Orville experienced weather conditions opposite to those Wilbur had experienced. Soon after the sailboat turned into Albemarle Sound, the wind died down to a whisper, reducing the boat's forward motion to a crawl. As a result it took sixteen long hours to cross the sound. But finally, on the morning of September 28, 1900, the sailboat slid up beside the small, deserted dock at Kitty Hawk.

Orville unloaded his trunk and baggage onto the dock. As he stood wondering where he would find Wilbur, an inquisitive boy wandered by. Orville called the boy over and commissioned him to go and find Wilbur and bring him to the dock.

Meanwhile Orville surveyed his new surroundings. The village of Kitty Hawk was located on the western side of the island, facing Albemarle Sound, and not the rough Atlantic Ocean that crashed ashore on the other side of the island. The village consisted of a couple of two-story dwellings, what looked like a store, and several single-story houses scattered among the marshy tidal woods. None of the structures were painted or well kept, and Orville could not help but compare them to the neat, freshly painted houses of West Dayton.

Twenty minutes after Orville's arrival at Kitty Hawk, Wilbur reached the dock on a horse-drawn cart. The two brothers greeted each other and then loaded Orville's luggage into the cart for the quarter-mile trip along a sandy road to the Tates' house. Along the way, Wilbur filled Orville in on the latest developments. He was pleased to report that assembly of the glider was almost complete.

"Wonderful," Orville said, looking around. "We chose this place in the hope that it would have wind, solitude, and soft sand, and it looks to me like we got all three!"

"We certainly did," Wilbur replied.

Soon the brothers arrived at the Tates' house, which happened to be one of the two-story houses Orville had spotted from the dock. The house was made of rough-hewn timber and had a wide veranda wrapped around it. Orville, though, was more interested in the canvas lean-to that Wilbur had pitched in the front yard, where Orville found the nearly completed glider and Mrs. Tate's sewing machine. Wilbur explained that he was nearly finished shortening and resewing the sateen fabric sheaths that would cover the shorter wings.

Moments later Addie Tate appeared on the veranda with two small girls hanging on to her skirt. Wilbur introduced her to his brother, and she insisted that Orville come inside for a meal. Inside the house was sparse. The walls were unpainted, and the house contained no books, no pictures on the walls, and very little furniture. But Orville felt right at home. Addie was as hospitable as Wilbur had said in his letter she was, and in no time she was busy fixing bacon and eggs for Orville. Soon her husband appeared at the house, carrying a wild goose he had just shot. Bill Tate quickly introduced himself to Orville, and the two of them fell into conversation. As they talked, Orville was surprised to discover that Bill was as caught up in the adventure of flying as Wilbur was.

Later, when the two brothers were outside once again, Wilbur told Orville that Bill was a most enthusiastic helper. Bill rushed through his work each morning so that he could spend the afternoon acting as Wilbur's assistant.

The next four days were spent erecting the tent Orville had brought with him and setting up camp. The brothers chose a site for their camp a few hundred yards south of the village of Kitty Hawk and dug a well for water. Since the well was shallow, they boiled enough water to drink every day. Both brothers remembered Orville's bout with typhoid four years earlier, and they did not wish to repeat the experience.

Soon the tent was pitched. The cots were set up on one side of it, and a small kitchen was set up on the other side. Orville designated himself the cook and arranged the canned vegetables, rice, and other staples he had brought with him on a shelf that Addie had loaned them. For his part, Wilbur agreed to be the dishwasher, not that the chore involved much washing. Since they had to boil all their water before they used it, the brothers tried to use as little of it as possible. As a result, Wilbur used sand to scour the pots, pans, and plates clean.

Once Wilbur and Orville had established the campsite and settled into their new domestic routine, they set to work finishing off the glider. When they were done, they moved the glider from the Tates' front yard to their campsite, where the tent they had erected was large enough to house it.

The nights grew colder as fall settled over the Outer Banks, and Orville was glad that he had brought extra blankets. It was often gusty, too, and although the tent was firmly anchored to a gnarled oak tree, sudden squalls often threatened to blow it down. As a result both brothers had to crawl out into pelting sandstorms to hold their tent down.

With the completion of the glider, Orville and Wilbur then turned their attention to building the wooden tower they intended to tether the glider to when they flew it. They chose a flat stretch of beach nearby their campsite on which to erect the tower, which would be fifteen feet high rather than the one hundred fifty feet tall that Wilbur had first envisaged it being.

By Saturday morning, one week after Orville's arrival, everything was ready. Orville tried to remain calm as he, Bill, and Wilbur carefully picked up the glider and carried it out of the tent and toward the tower. The men were careful to keep the front of it low so that it did not catch a sudden gust of wind and lift off.

Wilbur had borrowed a handheld anemometer from the local weather station, and he held it up to gauge the wind speed. "Twenty-five miles an hour," he yelled to Orville.

"A good wind for flying," Orville responded.

Before they hitched the glider to the tether rope from the tower, Wilbur wanted to get the feel of the new craft. He lay down in the cutaway section at the center of the bottom wing. His elbows rested on the leading edge of the wing, and with his hands he controlled the levers that altered the angle of the rudder at the front. His feet were pressed against the T-shaped lever that controlled the wing warping.

When Wilbur was comfortable, Orville and Bill lifted up the glider by its wing tips. When they got it to shoulder height, the wind caught the glider and lifted it into the air. Orville and Bill then let out ropes attached to the wing tips, and the glider climbed to a height of about fifteen feet. But as soon as it got to that height, the glider began to act erratically. The front of the craft would suddenly drop and then lift up again, and the glider rocked precariously from side to side. Despite Wilbur's best efforts at controlling the craft through warping the wings and adjusting the front rudder, nothing seemed to work. Finally Wilbur yelled above the wind to Orville, "Let me down! Let me down!"

Orville and Bill hauled in the ropes, and the glider settled onto the sand.

Orville asked his brother what was the matter, and Wilbur replied, "I promised Pop that I'd look after myself and not take any risks."

But Orville knew that there was more to it than that, and he guessed that Wilbur was a little shaken because the glider had not handled in the air the way the brothers had expected it to.

Wilbur regained his composure, and the three men attached the tether rope from the tower to the front of the glider. But Wilbur was unwilling to get back on the glider. Instead, they used a length of heavy chain that Bill had dragged down the beach from his house to simulate Wilbur's weight. Wilbur then attached ropes to the various control levers and prepared to control the glider from the ground. Something was not right from the start, however. The glider barely made it off the ground with the chain onboard. So the men halved the weight of the chain to seventy-five pounds and tried again. This time the glider rose easily into the air. But once again when it reached a height of about fifteen feet, it began to act erratically in the air. But the brothers persevered. They pulled the ropes and warped the wings and watched as the glider banked one way and then the other. And they tilted the angle of the rudder up and down. Despite all this, the craft still remained erratic in the air.

On those occasions when the glider remained steady in the air, Wilbur pointed out that the wings were not parallel to the ground at an angle of about three degrees as he had designed, but rather they were at an angle of about twenty degrees. And no matter what adjustments they made, the brothers could not seem to bring that angle down to anything less than ten degrees. Wilbur and Orville knew that the craft was off balance. The problem was, neither of them knew why.

Finally after about three hours of flying the glider, the brothers decided to call it a day. The test flight had given Orville and Wilbur more than enough to think about. The three men unhitched the craft from the tether rope and carried it back up the beach and stowed it in the tent.

That night Orville and Wilbur talked about the erratic behavior of the glider. Why was it behaving the way it did in the air? Was the curvature of the wing too shallow? After all, Wilbur had only guessed at the correct curvature. Was the wing surface area too small? Or was the fabric covering the wings too porous and allowing too much of the wind pressure to pass through the wings?

As they sat in their tent that night mulling over the problem, neither Orville nor Wilbur could come up with a reasonable explanation as to why the glider behaved the way it did in the air.

The following day was Sunday, and although the brothers did not like to attend church themselves, they never worked on Sunday out of respect for their father's beliefs. Instead they set out on a long walk to explore their surroundings. Bill and his nephew Tom joined them as they walked through the village. Word of the two brothers testing their glider had spread throughout the island, and as Wilbur and Orville walked along, the people they passed greeted them by saying, "Good afternoon, Mr. Wright and Mr. Wright."

Every house the men passed on the island had a small vegetable patch, though the produce growing in them was meager and spindly. Yet Orville was amazed. He wondered how anyone managed to coax vegetables to grow in the sandy soil.

"About sixty people live around Kitty Hawk," Bill said as they walked, "and most have several jobs. They fish in the summer, hunt bears and wild hogs in the fall and spring, and man the lifeguard stations in the winter. The stations are located every ten miles or so up and down the Outer Banks. They warn mariners of the dangerous shoals close to shore, and if a ship is wrecked, they do their best to rescue everyone. But if a northwester is blowing hard, that's a hard job, even for the most seasoned Outer Banker."

Bill looked deep in thought, as if he were recalling facts he had learned as a child thirty years before. Then he spoke again. "The Outer Banks have the longest European history. The Italian Verrazano cruised this coast in 1524, exploring for the French, and came ashore not far from this spot. He even kidnapped a local Indian and took the man back to present to the French court. I'll bet he had some tales to tell!

"And that's Roanoke Island, where the first English colony was set up in the New World." Bill pointed toward an island with a few pine trees on it just visible on the horizon. "They call it the Lost Colony, on account of its vanishing without a trace in 1588.

"Life here has always been about the sea. Most of us are here because our ancestors washed ashore on these islands. My father was a Scottish sailor who was shipwrecked here and never left."

"So shipwrecks were common?" Wilbur asked.

"Still are, but not as common as they used to be. They once called this the Graveyard of the Atlantic, and it wasn't all nature's doings, either. Nags Head and Jockey's Ridge are both named after eighteenth-century wreckers who used to lead horses with lamps around their necks along the top of the sand dunes. The bobbing lights tricked sea captains into thinking that there were ships at safe harbor and so lured them onto the treacherous shoals. Once a ship was wrecked, its cargo belonged to the first man who salvaged it. Many a living was made that way on the Outer Banks."

Ten-year-old Tom interrupted. "Don't forget about Blackbeard." Tom's eyes shined as he spoke. "He died at sea in a battle near here, and they chopped off his head. Then he jumped overboard without his head and swam around his ship three times before he sank to the bottom."

Orville reached over and patted Tom on his head. He had become fond of this young boy who told tall stories.

"What about the name Kitty Hawk? Where did that come from?" Orville asked.

Bill scratched his beard. "A bit hard to say, really," he replied, "though most folks here think it goes right back to an Indian name. There's an old map at the post office where the village is called Chickahawk, which probably turned into Kitty Hawk over time. One thing's for sure: there's no bird around here called a kitty hawk," he said, chuckling at his own joke.

The following day and for the next several days Orville and Wilbur continued testing their glider. They flew it with various weights of chain onboard. They flew it as a kite with the controls tied off, and they flew it with Wilbur controlling the craft by means of ropes tied to the control levers. They also flew the glider with a fish scale attached to the tether rope. In this way, using the anemometer to gauge the wind speed, they could note the amount of drag or resistance on the glider as it flew under various wind conditions. Wilbur carefully observed the craft in flight, trying to work out why it had a tendency to be unstable in the air, and he noted his observations and all the data he collected in a logbook for later study.

After three days Wilbur and Orville had to suspend their flying experiments with the glider because the weather had turned bad. Rain and high winds blustered across the Outer Banks, confining the two brothers to their tent, which nearly blew down on more than one occasion. Inside they studied the data they had collected so far and continued to search for an answer to the glider's erratic behavior in the air.

On the morning of October 10, Orville and Wilbur awoke to find that the rain had stopped and the wind had died down enough to continue tests with the glider. Once again, with Bill's help, they carried the craft out to the tower and attached it to the tether line. They flew the glider for several hours before hauling it in and detaching the tether line. The two brothers turned their backs on the craft for a few minutes while they discussed moving the tower to the top of Lookout Hill, a small rise just south of Kitty Hawk. As they discussed whether the wind there might be better for their purposes, a gust of wind burst across the island from the sea. It caught under one corner of the wing of the grounded glider and tossed the glider into the air. Orville and Wilbur spun around, but it was too late. The glider was already airborne. All the men could do was watch in horror as the glider slammed into the sand twenty feet away. The force of the impact smashed the right side of the glider, crushing the ribs, smashing the struts, and snapping the support wire that trussed the wing.

Dejected, Orville and Wilbur walked around the wreckage of their glider. Finally, as they hauled its twisted and broken hulk back to their tent, they talked about whether to pack up and head back to Dayton.

Chapter 7

Into the Air Again

That night as Orville lay on his cot, he thought over the conversation he'd had with his brother and wondered what they should do next. What had they achieved so far? The answer was not encouraging: the glider had been flown like a kite for a total of little more than three hours and for less than ten minutes with Wilbur aboard. And during that time Wilbur had discovered that it was difficult for a man to work the front rudder and wing-warping levers at the same time. Worse, as Wilbur had explained, the data they were gathering about lift and drag and correct angle of the wings contradicted the results derived from Otto Lilienthal's published equation and table of coefficients for lift and drag. The only conclusion Orville could draw from all this was that either they were wrong or Lilienthal was wrong. Neither conclusion was a happy one.

Yet Orville wondered whether they might not be on the edge of a breakthrough. But how would they ever know if they gave up now? As the early morning light filtered through the tent, Orville made up his mind that they should fix the glider and continue their flying experiments.

After breakfast the two brothers once again surveyed the wreckage of the glider. "I think we can patch it up," Orville commented. "We have enough tools with us to do the job, and we could borrow Mrs. Tate's sewing machine again to repair the ripped sateen covering."

Wilbur looked hopeful. "Last night I'd decided we should pack up and leave, but I think you're right. We should try again."

For the next hour Wilbur and Orville plotted how to go about fixing their flying contraption. The longer they talked, the more enthusiastic they became. It took them four days to repair the glider, splinting the broken ribs and struts together and repairing the torn fabric. The Wright brothers had no sooner finished the repair job than a fierce storm struck the Outer Banks. The weather station recorded it as a forty-five-mile-per-hour northeaster. The brothers tethered the glider firmly to the ground about fifty feet from the tent and sought shelter inside.

Orville had experienced many storms in Ohio, but never one where the wind picked up grains of sand and whipped them around like thousands of tiny bullets. The sand beat against the side of the tent, and the brothers could only imagine what was happening to their newly rebuilt glider.

In the two days it took for the storm to pass, Orville wrote several long letters, including one to Katharine in which he described his surroundings.

But the sand! The sand is the greatest thing in Kitty Hawk, and soon will be the only thing. The site of our tent was formerly a fertile valley, cultivated by some ancient Kitty Hawker. Now only a few rotten limbs, the topmost branches of trees that then grew in this valley, protrude from the sand. The sea has washed and the wind blown millions and millions of loads of sand up in heaps along the coast, completely covering houses and forest. Mr. Tate is now tearing down the nearest house to our camp to save it from the sand....

A mockingbird lives in a tree that overhangs our tent, and sings to us the whole day long. He is very tame, and perches on the highest bough of the tree (which however is only about ten feet high) and calls us up every morning. I think he crows up especially early after every storm to see whether we are still here....

The sunsets are the prettiest I have ever seen. The clouds light up in all colors in the background, with deep blue clouds of various shapes fringed with gold before. The moon rises in much the same style, and lights up this pile of sand almost like day. I read my watch at all hours of the night on moonless

nights without the aid of any other light than
that of the stars shining on the canvas of the
tent....

I believe I started to tell you what we eat.
Well, part of the time we eat hot biscuits and
eggs and tomatoes; part of the time eggs,
and part tomatoes. Just now we are out of
gasoline and coffee. Therefore no hot drink
or bread or crackers. The order sent off
Tuesday has been delayed by the winds. Will
is 'most starved. But he kept crying that
when we were rolling in luxuries, such as
butter, bacon, corn bread and coffee. I think
he will survive. It is now suppertime. I must
scratch around to see what I can get together.
We still have half a can of condensed milk,
which amounts to six or eight teaspoonfuls....

As soon as the wind died down, Orville climbed
out of the tent and went in search of the glider. One
lone wingtip poked out of the sand, and it took
Orville and Wilbur half the morning to dig the glider
out. Amazingly, the glider had not been damaged
by the storm. Later that day the brothers dragged
the craft to the nearest hilltop. They had decided to
abandon flying the kite tethered to the tower and
instead to fly it as a kite, each brother holding a
rope attached to the wingtips of the craft.

For the next two days Wilbur and Orville flew
the glider in a number of configurations. They flew
it with no weight aboard, and they flew it with the
heavy chain aboard. They flew it with the rudder set

at different angles, and they flew it with the rudder mounted on the back of the craft instead of the front. In every configuration in which they flew the glider, Orville and Wilbur studied the craft carefully in the air, making notes on how it handled under each condition.

Meanwhile Bill sailed to the mainland and brought back gasoline and coffee for the Wright brothers. A letter from Katharine also arrived. The news it bore was not good. Katharine explained that she had been forced to dismiss Harry Dillon, the young man whom Orville had left in charge of the bicycle shop.

In light of this development, Orville and Wilbur agreed that it was time for them to pack up and head for home—almost. They set the date for their departure from Kitty Hawk for Tuesday, October 23, to give themselves time to try flying the glider in free flight. Both Wilbur and Orville had come to the realization that to gather the information they needed on controlling a flying machine in the air, one of them had to climb back onto the glider and fly it free down a hillside as Otto Lilienthal had done.

On October 18, Orville and Wilbur carried the glider back out to the nearby sand hill. But by the time they got there, the wind had fallen to only ten miles per hour, not strong enough to hold the glider aloft with a man on it. Instead the brothers launched the glider from the top of the hill and watched it in free flight. Each time it hit the ground, they would retrieve it and carry it back to the top of the hill and launch it again. And if the glider was damaged when it crashed onto the sand at the end of the short flights, the brothers would repair the damage and fly it again. At the end of the day, they carried the glider back to camp and hoped that the wind would be stronger for a manned free flight the following day.

Sure enough, when Orville awoke the next morning, the wind had picked up. With Bill's help, Orville and Wilbur carried the glider four miles south down the beach from Kitty Hawk to Kill Devil Hills. But when they got there, Wilbur decided that this time the wind was too strong to safely make a manned flight. They tethered the glider to the ground and walked back to their camp at Kitty Hawk.

The next day the wind conditions were perfect for a manned flight. The brothers untethered the glider and carried it to the top of the hill. Wilbur then climbed aboard, lying facedown in the opening in the center of the bottom wing. Once he was in place, Orville and Bill picked up the glider by the wingtips and began to run down the hill. When they had gathered enough speed, Wilbur gave them a signal, and they launched the glider into the air. The glider then scooted down the side of the hill about three feet above the ground before finally coming to rest on the sand. The men then carried the glider back to the top of the hill and repeated the procedure. In all they made twelve flights this way, the longest lasting for about twenty seconds and covering four hundred feet.

It was a small beginning, but the flights taught Orville and Wilbur a lot about controlling the craft in the air. As Wilbur's earlier flight had demonstrated, controlling both the wing-warping mechanism and the rudder at the same time while the glider was in the air was no easy matter. But the brothers felt that they had enough data and experience to refine their glider design and improve the control mechanisms. They decided to leave the glider behind at Kill Devil Hills and return the following year with a redesigned glider to test.

On October 23, 1900, Wilbur and Orville Wright packed up their tent and belongings and said good-bye to Bill and Addie Tate and their two daughters. Addie was particularly interested to hear that the brothers had left the glider behind at Kill Devil Hills. She explained that she would like to use some of it. The struts could be chopped up for firewood during the winter, and the white sateen fabric covering the wings and rudder would make fine dresses for her daughters. Orville and Wilbur gladly gave her permission to salvage the glider.

As the boat pulled away from the dock in Kitty Hawk bound for Elizabeth City, Orville looked back at the beach and sand dunes. In the month he had spent at Kitty Hawk he had grown to love the rugged beauty of the place. But now it was time to go home and get the bicycle business back on track and to ponder what to do next in solving the problem of flying.

As the boat rocked gently back and forth as it made its way up Albemarle Sound, Wilbur broke into Orville's thoughts. "We have plenty to think about, Orv," he said. "We got only half the lift that Lilienthal's calculations said we should have gotten, and

I still can't work out why the drag was more than we had thought. But whatever else could have been, we can say we return to Ohio without having our pet theories completely knocked on the head by the hard logic of experience, and our own brains dashed out in the bargain."

"Yes indeed," Orville agreed. "At least we have lived to tell our story."

Chapter 8

Problems to Solve

Back in Dayton, Milton Wright welcomed his two sons home. Katharine was glad to see Wilbur and Orville as well. After their arrival home, the Wright brothers went back to work at the bicycle shop. As usual, while they worked, Wilbur and Orville talked over and considered the problems they had encountered flying their glider at Kitty Hawk.

On his return home, Wilbur wrote to Octave Chanute, telling him all about their fall adventure flying the glider. Chanute wrote back, telling the brothers how amazed he was that Wilbur had flown in the glider and urging them to be very careful in the future. He also encouraged them to write articles about their experiments with their glider.

Orville was particularly relieved when Wilbur agreed to do this, as he did not enjoy writing scientific articles. The two papers that Wilbur wrote were titled "Angle of Incidence," which appeared in the July 1901 issue of the British publication *The Aeronautical Journal,* and "The Horizontal Position During Gliding Flight," which appeared in a German aeronautical journal.

As the time to design a new glider to test at Kitty Hawk approached, Orville and Wilbur still had not answered the question of why the glider they had tested did not handle in the air as well as expected. Was the surface area of the wing too small, or did the problem lie with the curvature of the wing? Then one day Wilbur announced to Orville, "I think I have devised an experiment to test for an answer to our dilemma."

Over the next several days, as he continued to build new bicycles to sell during the coming spring and summer cycling season, Orville watched as Wilbur prepared his experiment.

Wilbur connected two lengths of wood to form a *V* shape. He attached the bottom of the *V* to a hinge that allowed it to pivot to the left or the right. Then he set to work on the next phase, making an array of model wings of different sizes and curvatures. When the model wings were prepared, he began his testing process. To the top of each piece of wood that formed the *V* shape he attached one of the wings. Then he observed the wing's performance in a constant breeze. The wing that was more aerodynamic was the one that moved up to a vertical position, pushing the other wing to the left or the right from its normal position.

The experiment was crude, Orville had to admit, but as Wilbur explained to him when he had finished testing, it answered their dilemma. "Lilienthal's figures for determining the surface area of a wing seem flawed. We need much more surface area for the glider to fly correctly and hold the weight of a man aloft with the required stability. But the test also seemed to hint that greater curvature of the wing will also help," Wilbur reported.

With this information in hand, Orville and Wilbur set to designing a new glider. The new glider would have a wingspan of twenty-two feet, and the wings would now be seven feet wide, giving the glider a total wing surface area of 308 square feet. The brothers also increased the curvature of the wings and moved the peak of the curve back slightly. This, according to their calculations, would cause the glider to fly with a five-degree angle of attack to the wind. The new glider would also be nearly twice as heavy as the previous one, weighing in at ninety-seven pounds.

By mid-May 1901, the plans for the new glider were complete. By now Orville and Wilbur were totally bitten by the flying bug, and nothing made them as happy as the thought of solving the problems of flight. In fact, the two brothers were so eager to test their new glider design that they decided not to wait until the fall to go to Kitty Hawk to test the craft. Instead they would go there during the summer months.

By the middle of June, Orville was bursting to get back to the remote island on the Outer Banks of

North Carolina. He and Wilbur employed a relative of their landlord's named Charles Taylor to take care of the bicycle shop in their absence. With this done, the brothers began to make the necessary final arrangements to head east for the summer.

As they busily fashioned the parts for the new glider which, like the previous one, they would assemble once they got to the Outer Banks, Orville sketched out plans for a large shed to be built at Kill Devil Hills. The brothers agreed that the new glider needed to be housed inside so that high winds or sandstorms would not damage the craft. The shed Orville planned to build was large enough to accommodate the twenty-two-foot wingspan of the glider. Both of the end walls of the structure were to be hinged so that they could be lifted up and propped open, allowing the shed to convert into a large tunnel. This would allow the brothers to lift the glider in and out of the shed more easily and to let cooling breezes blow through while they were assembling it. They planned to pitch a tent beside the shed for their living quarters.

This time Wilbur and Orville did not leave the buying of any of the supplies to chance. Orville visited a local timber yard and ordered lumber in the necessary length for the wing spars. And from a lumberyard in Elizabeth City, North Carolina, he sent ahead and ordered the timber, cut to length, for building the shed. He instructed that this timber be delivered to Kitty Hawk, to be waiting for them upon their arrival.

Before Orville and Wilbur left for North Carolina, an unexpected visitor arrived to see them—Octave

Chanute. The legendary old man of aeronautical science had come to Dayton to see for himself what the Wright brothers were up to. Orville and Wilbur were both delighted and daunted by his visit, and Katharine was thrown into a dither making sure the linen on the bed and the food she served their guest were perfect.

At the Wright house on Hawthorn Street, the three men talked late into the night about the problem of flight. In the course of the conversation, Chanute mentioned that he knew of two men who might be able to help Orville and Wilbur. The first man was Edward Huffaker, who held a master's degree in physics. Chanute explained that he had commissioned Edward to make a glider for him. The other man was George Spratt, and although he had no real practical experience with gliders, Chanute liked his ideas and enthusiasm and thought he would be a good addition to any flying team.

When Orville heard the word *team,* he cringed. He and Wilbur were already a great team. They understood each other perfectly and sparred together until they found scientific answers to problems that satisfied them both. Orville did not feel the need for the help of anyone else, and he was sure that Wilbur did not either. However, since the great Octave Chanute was in their dining room, asking whether the two men could join them at Kitty Hawk, Orville felt obliged to offer an invitation.

Later, when he discussed the situation with Wilbur, Orville learned that his brother did indeed feel the same way about the matter. But it would have been rude of them to say that the two men could not come along to Kitty Hawk. All Orville and Wilbur could do was hope that the two visitors would be helpful. They would find out soon enough.

On July 7, 1901, Orville and Wilbur began the trip east to North Carolina. The parts for the new glider and their baggage were loaded aboard the train with them. To their surprise they arrived in Elizabeth City the following day just as a hurricane blew into town. No one knew precisely how strong the winds were blowing, because the gauges had been ripped apart after registering wind gusts of ninety-three miles per hour.

When the hurricane finally passed, Orville and Wilbur were able to charter a boat and cross Albemarle Sound to Kitty Hawk, where they were welcomed once again by Bill Tate and his family. They stayed the night with the Tates, battling bedbugs, and were grateful to set off for Kill Devil Hills the following morning.

The brothers chose a site at Kill Devil Hills and set up the tent that would serve as their living quarters. The precut wood had been delivered to the barrier island, and the brothers got to work constructing the wooden shed. They had nearly finished the job when Edward Huffaker arrived at camp. Edward did not make a good first impression, complaining about everything he could think of and not offering to help with either preparing the meals or washing the dishes. That same day the camp was inundated with mosquitoes. Both Orville and Wilbur had never seen anything like it—nor did they ever want to again. The sky filled with black swarms of the insects, and the men soon discovered that the mesh of their mosquito nets was too course and failed to keep the onslaught away from them. No matter what they did, the three men could not escape. On the first night they went to bed at five o'clock, wrapping themselves in blankets so that just their noses protruded. But they soon got unbearably hot and had to uncover themselves, leading to another round of mosquito bites.

No one slept much that night, or the following night, and tempers wore thin. Wilbur and Orville liked Edward even less the second day. Orville dressed impeccably, even on a remote sand dune, while Edward cared little about how he looked, wearing the same shirt for a second day. In fact, the shirt smelled so bad that Orville imagined that he had probably worn it on the whole trip to Kill Devil Hills. Nor did Edward seem to care much about the precious scientific equipment, leaving Wilbur's micrometer in the sand and using the camera box as a footstool.

The following night the men dragged driftwood back to their campsite and made a smoky fire. Although the smoke helped keep the mosquitoes away, it caused everyone to cough and splutter through the night.

On July 26 George Spratt arrived, and unlike their first visitor, the Wright brothers enjoyed his company from the start.

Despite the mosquitoes, lack of sleep, and the hot, humid weather, Orville and Wilbur managed to erect the wooden shed and completed assembly of the glider the day after George arrived. With the glider complete, their excitement grew as they antic- ipated flying it.

Finally, on Saturday, July 27, with the help of Edward and George, Orville and Wilbur carried the glider up the large sand dune to test it out. They had hoped to fly it as a kite, but since the wind was not strong enough, Wilbur volunteered to pilot it on a downhill glide.

Wilbur stretched himself out in the recess at the center of the bottom wing and prepared himself for the first flight. When he signaled that he was ready, the three other men picked up the glider and began to run down the side of the sand hill. When they had gathered enough speed, Wilbur gave the sign and they launched the glider into the air. However, the glider did not go very far before it nose-dived into the sand. The men carried the glider back up the hill. This time Wilbur shuffled his weight back a few inches in the recess to try to shift the center of balance and keep the nose of the glider up. Once again Orville, Edward, and George launched the craft, and once again the nose began to drop. On the third flight Wilbur shuffled his body back one foot to improve the balance of the glider. He could barely reach the control sticks of the front rudder (elevator). This time the glider did not nose-dive into the sand but rather undulated in the air as Wilbur sought to keep the craft level.

In all they made about nineteen flights in the glider that day. On one of the flights, the glider cov- ered a distance of 315 feet in twenty seconds.

Huffaker was very excited about the flight; it was the farthest he had ever seen anyone glide. But Orville could tell that Wilbur was not happy with the performance of the glider, and with good reason. On every flight the craft had undulated in the air as it flew, leaving Wilbur fighting the rudder control to keep it level. And on two of the flights the nose had risen precariously into the air, almost causing the glider to stall out in the air and crash to the ground. It was only the quick thinking of Wilbur, throwing his weight forward and altering the center of balance, that stopped such a crash from happening. Orville knew that that was exactly the type of crash that had taken the life of Otto Lilienthal.

"Something's wrong with the glider. It's not handling like it should," Wilbur confessed to Orville after they had stowed the glider back into its wooden hangar. "The wings are producing only about a third of the expected lift, and I'm having to use the rudder far more to keep the nose up or down than I had to on last year's glider. And given the size of the rudder, it's easy to overcorrect, adding to the control problem."

The two brothers talked long into the night about the problem, and Wilbur made copious notes in a log. The following day they reduced the size of the rudder (elevator) to ten square feet in an attempt to make it a little less responsive, hoping to reduce the tendency of overcorrecting Wilbur had noted.

Once they had reduced the size of the rudder, the four men carried the glider back up the sand hill, where Wilbur made more test flights. The smaller rudder did indeed decrease the tendency to over-correct, but the glider was still not stable in the air. Sometimes the nose rose unexpectedly, and some-times, especially when the wind speed picked up, it nosed downward.

That night Wilbur and Orville talked more about the problem. Somehow the center of air pressure on the wings was shifting forward and backward on the wings, throwing the glider off balance and causing the nose to rise or fall.

"What if we remove the top wing and fly it as a kite?" Orville suggested. "That way we can observe it closely in the air in a variety of wind conditions and see how it responds."

"That's a good idea," Wilbur replied.

The following day, with the help of their two guests, the Wright brothers detached the top wing and carried the glider to the top of the sand hill. There Orville attached two ropes to it, and the men launched it and flew it as a kite.

As Orville had suggested, this procedure proved very enlightening. At fairly low wind speed, the back of the wing dropped, causing the wing to fly at an increased angle to the wind. As the wind speed picked up, the angle of attack decreased, and the wing flew almost horizontal to the ground. But in winds above twenty-five miles per hour the front edge of the wing began to dip at a negative angle to the wind, causing the wing to race toward the ground as Orville and Wilbur tugged at the tether ropes to stop it from crashing. The men also observed that this wing presented a lot more resistance to the wind than did the wings of the glider of the year before.

The Wright brothers' suspicions were confirmed. The center of pressure was moving backward and forward on the wing, depending upon the velocity of the wind, and making the glider unstable as its nose pitched up and down.

That night, as the brothers sat outside by a fire, Wilbur explained to Orville that he thought the stability problem lay in the curvature of the wing. It was too great, which in turn created a lot of drag. Depending upon the wind speed, this moved the center of pressure backward or forward. Orville nodded. He had come to the same conclusion.

The following morning the brothers set to work modifying the curvature of the glider wings. They laid long spars lengthwise across each wing from wingtip to wingtip. When these spars were tightened down, they began to flatten the ribs that gave the wing its shape, reducing the camber, or curvature, of the wing in the process. Orville and Wilbur also altered the leading edge of the wing to make its shape more like that of the glider from the year before.

On August 5, while Wilbur and Orville were in the midst of making the alterations to their glider, Octave Chanute arrived at camp. As he talked with the Wright brothers, he was soon impressed with how far they had come in their flying experiments. Orville chuckled to himself as Edward raved on about his and Wilbur's mechanical abilities and the fact that they had already managed to fly the glider a distance of over three hundred feet. But Orville did not let the praise go to his head. The brothers may have flown that distance, but the glider had not flown as they had intended. Despite a problem with the glider's pitch control, they were hopeful that the modifications they were making would fix the problem. Yet Orville was sure that there would be more theoretical problems to overcome once they got the glider back in the air.

On Thursday, August 8, the modifications to the glider were complete, and Wilbur, Orville, Edward, and George carried the craft out of its hangar and back up the sand dune, with Octave Chanute trotting along behind them. The men flew the glider again, and this time, much to Orville's relief, Wilbur reported that longitudinal, or pitch control, was greatly improved. As a result during one of the flights that day, the glider covered a distance in the air of nearly four hundred feet. Chanute was most impressed, informing the Wright brothers that covering that distance had set a new distance record for gliding.

With the pitch-control problem under control, Orville and Wilbur decided it was time to experiment with the wing-warping mechanism, attempting both to control the glider roll in the air and to turn the craft in flight. On this glider they had replaced the T-shaped foot controller—which Wilbur had found to be counter-intuitive and hard to use—with a hip cradle device. When Wilbur felt the left wing dip in flight, he would shift his hips to the right, activating wing warping in the opposite direction to the dip and restoring the glider to even balance in the air.

Orville watched from the side of the sand hill as Wilbur flew the glider and activated the wing warping. From Orville's position everything seemed to go according to plan, but Wilbur did not think so. "There's something wrong. The machine has a peculiar feeling of instability when I warp the wings," he reported to Orville at the end of the flight.

But Wilbur was too preoccupied with all the other things involved in flying the glider to notice exactly what the problem was. The only thing for Wilbur to do was to make several more flights so that he could try to concentrate on the problem.

During these flights Wilbur was able to isolate the feeling of instability when he attempted to warp the wings. He explained to Orville that at first everything felt normal: one wing would dip, and the other would rise as the glider banked into a turn. But then it began to feel as if the wing that was angled up wanted to turn in the other direction, as if the craft wanted to spin in the opposite direction around the center of the turn direction. It was a strange and disorienting feeling.

Then on one of the flights, as Wilbur attempted to warp the wings, the tip of one of the wings hit the ground, causing the glider to crash onto the sand. The force of the impact sent Wilbur reeling forward from his prone position in the recess of the bottom wing and crashing through the rudder. Orville ran to his brother as fast as he could. He found Wilbur shaken and his face cut and bruised, but thankfully no bones had been broken in the crash.

Orville repaired the glider's broken rudder, and the following day the brothers decided to fly the glider as a kite, rather than risk more disaster with Wilbur on it, while they investigated the new control problem. Using ropes attached to control the wing-warping mechanism, Wilbur and Orville closely observed the glider in the air. After several days of flying the glider in this manner, they began to observe the problem. When the wings were warped and the glider banked into a turn, it was not long before the wing that was banked upward began to fall behind, causing the craft to skid or try to turn in the opposite direction, confirming the feeling that Wilbur had earlier reported.

While Wilbur and Orville were still pondering the problem, Chanute left camp for home on August 11. Chanute told the brothers that despite the latest problem, he was very impressed with how far they had come in solving the problem of flight.

As Orville and Wilbur continued to fly the glider as a kite and brainstorm about the problem they were experiencing, they finally came to an under-standing of what was going on. When the wings were warped and the glider began to turn, the wing tilted up was encountering more wind resistance, causing it to slow down, while the wing tilted in the opposite direction remained at a constant speed. As the upper wing slowed more and more from the increased resistance, it wanted to turn in the direc-tion of the resistance and away from the direction of the turn. If this was allowed to continue, the glider would eventually tumble from the sky and crash like a bird with a broken wing.

That was the problem. The only trouble was, neither Wilbur nor Orville could think of a solution. By the time the Wright brothers left Kitty Hawk on

August 22, 1901, to return to Dayton, Orville was feeling discouraged. One look at his brother confirmed that Wilbur felt the same way. Talking together on the boat trip back across Albemarle Sound to Elizabeth City cemented their gloom. The two brothers agreed that it was probably time for them to give up their dreams of flying. Although they had broken the record for distance in gliding during this trip and had impressed the great Octave Chanute with their efforts, they considered their experiments futile. "Man will learn to fly someday," Wilbur predicted gloomily, "but it won't be within our lifetime. There are just too many unknown problems to overcome."

Orville nodded in agreement, thankful that they had not wasted any more of their time or money on such a hopeless pursuit. It was time to get back to Dayton and revitalize their bicycle business.

Chapter 9

Breakthroughs

"You'll never guess what has happened," Wilbur said, turning the letter over in his hands. "Mr. Chanute has arranged for me to speak before the Western Society of Engineers in Chicago."

"Wonderful," Katharine interjected as she cleared away the lunch dishes.

"I'm not so sure," Wilbur replied. "He's already set the date for September 18, only three weeks away. And he wants me to bring as many lantern slides as I can. Would that be possible, Orv?"

Orville thought for a minute. He had a box full of undeveloped glass plates. Turning them into lantern slides was a delicate and time-consuming job. "I think I could do it," he finally said, "if Katharine wouldn't mind giving up the kitchen for a couple of days. I could put blankets over the windows and make an effective darkroom."

"Even so, I'm not sure I want to go," Wilbur replied. "It seems so sudden, and we have no idea what went wrong with the flying experiments this summer. I could make a complete fool of myself, especially if they ask questions I can't answer."

"Nonsense!" Katharine said. "It will give you the chance to get acquainted with some scientific men, and it may do you a lot of good."

A long silence followed. Orville knew that this was a pivotal moment for them. If Wilbur accepted the speaking engagement, they would have to work day and night to sift through the data they had collected to solve the puzzle of what had gone wrong and how they might correct it. But if Wilbur did not accept the invitation, they would go back to their bicycle business and forget about flying.

It was the following day before Wilbur decided that he would go to Chicago and tell the group of prestigious engineers what he knew about aerodynamics and the art of flying.

Once the decision was made, the household was taken over by the upcoming event. Orville and Wilbur worked tirelessly to arrange and interpret the data they had collected while Katharine bustled around trying to find the perfect suit for Wilbur to wear. In the end she decided he should wear one of Orville's outfits, since Orville was by far the more meticulous dresser.

Finally, on September 17, everything was ready. Carrying a bag of lantern slides, Wilbur left for Chicago. Since the brothers had had no breakthroughs in their understanding of how to correct the problem they had encountered that summer in Kitty Hawk, they decided that Wilbur should stick with the facts they had gathered.

Apparently that was enough, because Wilbur arrived back three days later full of enthusiasm. Octave Chanute wanted the entire text of the speech Wilbur had given to be published in the *Western Society of Engineers* journal, and he had even offered to pay the Wright brothers to continue their work with flying machines.

Much to Orville's relief, Wilbur explained that he had rejected the offer, partly because neither of them had any idea what to do next. They still felt sure that Lilienthal's tables for the coefficients of lift and drag, used to derive results from his equations and used by most flying experimenters, were wrong. But Orville and Wilbur did not know how to disprove them.

As the two brothers walked together to the bicycle shop a week later, a chance conversation set them on the right path in the quest to solving the problem of flight.

"According to Lilienthal, if you take a cambered wing of one square foot in surface area and set it at a five-degree angle of attack, the lift generated by this wing should equal the pressure on a .66 of a square foot metal plate set at a ninety-degree angle to the wind," Wilbur muttered, as much to himself as to Orville as they walked along.

"What we need is a way to measure that and see whether it's true—some device that can rotate freely in the wind," Orville replied.

"Like a bicycle wheel mounted horizontally," Wilbur said.

Suddenly the two brothers stopped dead in their tracks and looked at each other. It was such a simple and straightforward solution! Why hadn't they thought of it sooner?

At the bicycle store Wilbur and Orville set to work, and by the next day, the contraption was ready to begin experimenting with. The brothers had horizontally mounted a bicycle wheel on a hub above the handlebars so that it could turn freely. Mounted vertically at the twelve-o'clock position on the wheel was a metal plate curved to the curvature that Lilienthal had stated for his wing design. This plate was set at a five-degree angle to the wind. At the nine-o'clock position was mounted a smaller, flat metal plate set perpendicular to the airflow. When the bike was pedaled, it would create airflow over the curved plate, which would produce lift and turn the wheel in a clockwise direction. However, the force of the wind hitting the flat metal plate would offset the force of the lift. If Lilienthal's numbers were correct, the wheel would not turn but would stay steady with the metal plates in the nine-o'clock and twelve-o'clock positions. But if his figures were not correct and there was too much lift, the wheel would move clockwise. And if there was too much drag, the wheel would move counterclockwise.

Wilbur and Orville took turns pedaling the bike as fast as they could up and down the street in front of the bicycle store. Their antics soon gathered an amused group of onlookers, whom Orville could only imagine were wondering what crazy scheme the Wright brothers were up to this time.

The experiment proved to be a success. Lilienthal's figures for the coefficient of lift and drag were wrong. Instead of staying put as it should have, the wheel moved counterclockwise, indicating that there was too much drag and not enough lift. Only after they had considerably altered the angle of the curved plate to the wind could the brothers get the wheel to stay balanced.

Now, more than ever before, Orville and Wilbur were absorbed in their work. Both of them sensed that they were on the verge of a breakthrough, and that breakthrough might well help them to unravel the problem of flight—something man had dreamed of since the dawn of time.

With the new information from the bicycle wheel experiment in hand, Orville and Wilbur decided that it was time to build their own wind tunnel to test various wing designs and gather data that they could rely on in designing their next glider. (The first wind tunnel had been employed thirty years before, and Orville and Wilbur had read about it in one of the flying publications.)

First the brothers constructed a box six feet long, with inside measurements of sixteen inches by sixteen inches. They mounted the box on wooden legs at either end. A propeller carved from a single piece of wood provided the wind for the tunnel. The single-cylinder engine that Wilbur and Orville had built to run the machine tools at the bicycle shop turned the propeller. On the top of the box was a square hole, over which was placed a sheet of glass. Below the glass, bolted to the bottom of the box, was a precise balance delicately constructed from bicycle-spoke wire and hacksaw blades. The balance was designed to measure the lift and drag of the various wing forms vertically attached to it. Looking down through the glass, the brothers would be able to read the results that registered on a quadrant at the bottom of the balance.

By late November 1901 the wind tunnel was complete, and Wilbur and Orville installed it in the upstairs room at the bicycle shop. Once the contraption was placed there, none of the furniture could be moved. To ensure that conditions in the room remained exactly the same for every test they conducted, the brothers had to stand in the exact same place each time they operated the wind tunnel.

By now winter had begun to settle over Ohio, and few customers were coming to the bicycle store, allowing Orville and Wilbur to retreat to the upstairs room and begin their testing. The brothers made various wings from pieces of sheet metal, each one curved slightly differently than the previous one. Sometimes they used solder and wax to increase the thickness of the leading edge of the wing. Each wing shape was placed on the balance in the wind tunnel and tested at fourteen different angles of attack to the wind. The brothers noted the measurement of lift and drag at each angle for the particular wing and jotted down the results in a notebook before moving on to test the next wing.

When they had finally finished their testing, Wilbur and Orville had generated their own set of tables for the lift and drag coefficients of each wing shape. They had also discovered that the best-shaped wing, providing the most lift and least drag, was a parabolic curve, with the arch of the curve a quarter of the way back on the wing from the leading edge.

In the process of their experiments, Orville and Wilbur discovered that the standard figure they were using for the coefficient of air pressure was wrong. This alone helped to explain why the wings of their two gliders had produced only about a third of the lift expected. It took several days of calculating, but eventually the brothers were able to derive a smaller, more precise coefficient for air pressure.

With these new data in hand, the brothers set about designing a new glider to test in the fall of 1902 at Kitty Hawk. As much as Orville would have liked to have devoted all his time to developing the new glider, he and Wilbur had to busy themselves building new bicycles to sell during the upcoming spring and summer biking season.

In late August 1902, leaving Charles to run the bicycle shop, Orville and Wilbur set out for Kitty Hawk for a third time. As before, they carried with them all the parts and pieces they would need to assemble their new glider once they arrived on the Outer Banks.

When Orville and Wilbur got to Kitty Hawk, Bill Tate and his family once again welcomed them to the island and helped them to transfer all of the

glider parts and baggage to the campsite at Kill
Devil Hills. The hangar the men had built the year
before was battered but still standing, and Orville
began making repairs to it. Determined to upgrade
their living conditions this year, Orville also added
an extension to the back of the wooden hangar to
provide a kitchen and living quarters.

To furnish the new living quarters, Orville had
brought tablecloths, crockery, and upholstered
chairs. He had also brought along a whole trunk of
food to stock the kitchen. Orville positioned the food
on the shelf he had built in the new kitchen for that
purpose. When he was done, he looked at the
stocked shelf with great satisfaction. This summer
he and Wilbur would have canned peaches, pine-
apples, apples, and vegetables to eat, and they had
ample supplies of such items as coffee, sugar, flour,
spices, and cooking oil. In addition, this year the
Wright brothers were not going to sleep on creaky,
uncomfortable cots. Instead they constructed two
beds for themselves in the rafters of the hangar. The
beds were made of heavy burlap stretched over a
wooden frame. Orville also built a ladder to get up to
their new beds.

Once their new living quarters were in order,
Wilbur and Orville set to work building the glider.
They salvaged the wing struts from the 1901 glider,
which was no longer needed. Using the struts and
the other parts they had brought with them, the
brothers began assembling the wings for the new
glider.

The wings of the new glider were very different
from the wings of the previous two the brothers had

tested at Kitty Hawk. Based on the brothers' findings from the wind-tunnel experiments, the new wings were longer and narrower. Like the previous gliders, this one had an elevator mounted on the front. But unlike the other gliders, this version also had two fixed vertical rudders mounted at the back. This had been Orville's design innovation. Orville believed that the two rudders would help offset the tendency of the glider to want to turn back on itself during turns while the wings were warped.

By September 19, 1902, construction of the glider was complete. This glider was considerably heavier than its predecessors, weighing in at 116 pounds. Wilbur and Orville needed Bill's help to lift it out of the hangar and lug it up the side of a sand dune. At the top of the dune, they first flew their new glider as a kite. They were impressed with the way it handled in the air. The wing provided lots of lift, and the craft flew at an almost horizontal level.

After flying the glider as a kite, Wilbur climbed aboard and took the controls for a free flight. Orville watched as his brother soared down the side of the sand dune. When the glider finally came to rest on the sand, Wilbur jumped off and told Orville how much easier this glider was to fly than the previous ones.

Over the next several days, Wilbur made numerous flights in the glider, each time gliding farther and farther until he was surpassing the distance he had covered the year before. And when he warped the wings to keep them on an even line or to make a turn, he noted that Orville's rudders seemed to help overcome the difficulties of the year before. He reported to Orville, however, that on a couple of occasions while warping the wings, the craft seemed to want to spin in the direction of the wing that was angled down. But generally the glider handled well in the air.

Two days of heavy rain stopped the brothers' flying experiments with the new glider. But when the rain finally ceased and they could take to the air again, Wilbur announced to Orville that it was time for him to learn to fly.

Wilbur gave his brother some pointers on handling the glider in the air, and then Orville climbed into the pilot's recess in the bottom wing. He slipped his hips into the cradle that controlled the wing warping and gripped the levers that operated the front elevator. Wilbur and Bill hoisted the craft up and began running down the side of the sand dune before launching it into the air. Suddenly Orville was free, soaring above the dunes. The wind blustered against his face; it was a feeling he would not forget. At first he made a number of straight-line flights, not using the wing-warping controls until he got a feel for the glider and how it handled in the air. It was all very exhilarating, and soon Orville felt confident enough to start warping the wings to keep them on an even keel and to make turns.

On one of his flights Orville was soaring about thirty feet above the ground. As he began to make a turn, he noticed that the wing that was angled up was getting too high and the glider was about to go into a spin. He struggled with the wing-warping control to try to even out the glider in the air, but he forgot to change the angle of the front elevator to bring the glider's nose down. The front of the glider reared up until the craft came to a standstill in the air. Orville that knew he was in trouble. He spun his head around to see that the glider was falling backward toward the ground. He was going to crash, he could do nothing about it except brace himself for the impact. As the glider smashed hard against the sand, Orville could hear the sound of snapping wood as the wing struts and trusses splintered on impact.

"Orv? Orv, are you all right?" Wilbur asked between pants as he ran to the site of the crash.

"I think I'm fine," Orville replied, "which is more than I can say for the glider."

Wilbur helped Orville to get out from among the wreckage. Luckily Orville did not suffer even a cut or a bruise in the crash. Once he was back on his feet, he surveyed the broken glider. "It can be put back together," he announced, "but it's going to take a little time."

In fact it took the Wright brothers almost a week to repair their glider. And while he was glad that he suffered no serious injuries in the crash, Orville was baffled by the accident. What had happened to cause the glider to want to go into a spin? He pondered the question again and again. Then one night as he lay awake in his bed, he had an insight. Could it be that the glider had wanted to go into a spin because there was no way to alter the angle of the rudders at the back of the glider in relation to the wings? Yes! Orville told himself that he had solved the last great hindrance to controlling an aircraft in the air. The tail rudders had to be movable like the wings so that they could adjust to changes in the wind and balance out the forces of lift and drag as the glider was turning.

There was no sleep for the rest of the night for Orville, who spent the hours designing the new movable tail in his head. By the time the sun rose, Orville could hardly wait to describe his solution to Wilbur.

"You're right!" Wilbur said, slapping his knee. "Of course! We should have seen that sooner. It's the breakthrough we've been looking for." He took a couple of sips of coffee, and then his eyes lit up. "And we should simplify the whole thing by connecting the tail rudder controls to the cradle that controls the wing warping. That way the two of them could move together. And it wouldn't take any more effort to control the two systems from the cradle, though it would be easier to rig if we replaced the two tail rudders with one single, larger rudder."

"Absolutely," Orville replied, glad to see such a happy gleam in his big brother's eyes. "And I've been thinking about how we can hinge the tail rudder."

For the rest of that day, and the following day as well, the Wright brothers worked away, altering the tail rudder and rigging the new controls to adjust its angle in flight.

Just when they were getting ready to fly the rebuilt and modified glider again, Octave Chanute arrived at the camp at Kill Devil Hills, accompanied by his assistant, Augustus Herring. The men brought a huge wooden box with them and informed Orville and Wilbur that it contained a triwinged glider that Chanute had designed.

Orville was particularly frustrated when he learned that Chanute expected him and Wilbur to help Herring fly his glider. Despite his frustration, since Orville did not want to appear rude, he agreed to help, and on October 6 the triwinged glider took to the air. The flight was short: the glider covered just twenty feet before the right wing broke and the glider fell to the ground. Fortunately no one was hurt in the crash, but Chanute's and Herring's hopes were dashed.

It now occurred to Orville and Wilbur that their mentor, the eminent scientist and engineer, did not understand as much about flying as they did. However, they were far too polite to suggest this to Chanute, and they graciously accepted the man's offer of the broken glider, which Chanute had decided would be "very useful" to them.

After Chanute and Herring left the camp at Kill Devil Hills, Orville and Wilbur busied themselves flying their glider from dawn to dusk. The modifications made to the tail rudder worked perfectly. The brothers had finally worked out all the pieces of the control problem and could now control their glider along all three axes: pitch, roll, and yaw. Soon Wilbur and Orville were making flights in excess of five hundred feet. And on October 23, 1902, Wilbur covered 622 feet in twenty-six seconds in the glider, a new time and distance record for gliding, and Orville flew 615 feet in twenty-one seconds. Orville could not have been happier.

On October 28, 1902, Wilbur and Orville left the Outer Banks of North Carolina for home. But this time they left Kitty Hawk feeling triumphant. They had solved the puzzle of how to control the glider in three dimensions, and they had built a glider that for once produced the amount of lift they had antici- pated. Now it was time to think about building a powered flying machine. Of course there were lots of technical issues yet to be solved in producing such a machine, but Orville and Wilbur were sure that they could solve them. It was time for the Wright brothers to really take to the skies!

Chapter 10

The Flyer

When Orville and Wilbur arrived back in Dayton, they found that Charles was taking excellent care of their bicycle business. This allowed the brothers to focus on designing a new powered flying machine to fly at Kitty Hawk the following summer. As they began this process, they needed to concentrate on three basic areas. The first was a lightweight engine to power the craft. The second, a propeller to move the machine in the air. The third was a new airframe that integrated their latest discoveries regarding flight controls, was sturdy enough to support an engine, and generated enough lift to get all of the added weight into the air.

The brothers' first concern was an engine. They needed one that would produce eight or nine horsepower and weighed no more than about two hundred pounds. They hunted for a suitable motor, and although they followed every lead, they could not find anyone who felt capable of producing such an innovative engine. The brothers seemed to have no other choice but to set about making their own engine.

Both Orville and Wilbur understood how an engine worked. After all, they had pieced together the single-cylinder stationary engine that powered the machine tools in the bicycle shop. But this new engine needed to have four cylinders and had to be lighter than any other engine built so far. To help them in this endeavor, they conscripted Charles Taylor. And although Charles was not overly familiar with engines, admitting that he had attempted but failed to repair an automobile engine two years before, he was an excellent machinist and would be able to fashion the precise pieces needed for the engine.

Once they had the basic design for the engine, the brothers employed a foundry to cast the new engine block in aluminum to save weight. When the engine block arrived, Charles bored out the four cylinders on the lathe. He then set to making the crankshaft and pistons and rings to go into the engine.

While Charles worked away building the engine, Orville and Wilbur embarked on designing and constructing two propellers for their flying machine. They thought this would be a much simpler task than it turned out to be. The brothers had assumed that the propeller of a flying machine would work much like the propeller on a ship. But when they went to the library in Dayton to research data on the design of ship propellers, they discovered that no one had worked out a theory of efficient propeller design. Ship propellers, they learned, were designed by trial and error for each ship they were fitted to. This left Orville and Wilbur scratching their heads. If they could find no theory for building an efficient propeller, they were going to have to come up with a theory of their own.

It took more than two months, but eventually the brothers came to a theoretical understanding of how the propeller of a flying machine would work. Essentially the propeller was like a vertically mounted wing of a flying machine that spiraled through the air. Since it had the same curved shape as a wing, the spinning propeller generated lift. And because it was mounted vertically, instead of holding the flying machine aloft, the propeller pushed the machine forward in the air. With this understanding, Orville and Wilbur went back and studied the results from their wind-tunnel tests with various wing shapes to find the most efficient shape for their propeller. Once they had established this, they set to work designing the propellers.

In early January 1903, Octave Chanute set sail for Europe as an ambassador for the St. Louis World's Fair to be held the following year. He informed Wilbur and Orville that while he was in France, he intended to make a speech to the prestigious Aero Club about their aeronautical breakthroughs. Although the Wright brothers did not have any patents yet, they were not overly concerned about this. For one thing, Chanute was now seventy years old, and the new technology Orville and Wilbur were developing had passed him by. They knew that Chanute did not really understand their wing-warping system and therefore could not explain it properly to anyone else.

The other reason the brothers were not concerned about Chanute's revealing their flying breakthroughs was that the French were woefully behind in the race to build a manned, powered, heavier-than-air flying machine. Once the French had led the world in flight. In the 1780s, over 120 years before, they had developed the hot-air balloon and had continued to lead the world in lighter-than-air flight. By 1800 the whole of France had been swept by the ballooning craze, and rich men and women regularly attended "aerial picnics" in balloons above the countryside. And in November 1902 a French dirigible was flown for twenty-five miles, a new record in lighter-than-air flight. But since the German Otto Lilienthal's untimely death in 1896, no French scientists had seriously pursued heavier-than-air flight.

While the French were not a threat, Wilbur and Orville were concerned about Americans copying their ideas. They decided it was time to patent their flying technology, as it was only a matter of time before it was copied. Wilbur took the lead in the process, painstakingly drawing their inventions and writing accounts of how they worked. The Wright brothers sent off their patent applications with high hopes, only to have them dashed several weeks later.

An attorney from the patent office wrote to inform the Wright brothers that the office did not accept applications for inventions that did not work. He explained that in the past fifty years the office had been receiving a steady stream of patent applications for fanciful flying machines, and inspectors in the office had not taken a serious look at any of them. What was more, according to the attorney, nothing in the Wright brothers' paper work suggested anything but another wild dream.

Both Wilbur and Orville were shocked to be dismissed so lightly, and Wilbur refiled the patent applications, taking even more care to spell out their inventions in detail. They received back from the patent office a no-nonsense letter telling them not to apply again unless they used a skilled attorney who knew how to represent them. By then, however, the brothers had other, more important things on their minds.

By mid-February 1903 the new engine was ready to test. Orville, Wilbur, and Charles gathered around the engine as it sputtered to life. It worked! The following day, however, when they tried to start it again, some gasoline dripped onto a bearing, and the engine seized, splitting the engine block. The block could not be repaired, and Charles started work on a replacement engine.

Six weeks later the engine was complete. This time there were no glitches, and Wilbur measured the engine's output to be between twelve and sixteen horsepower, more than enough to lift and propel their flying machine.

The previous glider had used a wing surface area of about three hundred square feet, but the wings of the new flying machine, which they dubbed the "Flyer," were going to be two hundred square feet, and the whole machine would be heavier. Orville estimated that the Flyer, with larger wings and an engine, would weigh at least 625 pounds. And if everything went according to plan, it should fly at twenty-three miles per hour.

By June 1903 the end was in sight, and Orville sat down at Katharine's desk to write a letter to George Spratt. Originally he had only intended to invite George to Kitty Hawk later in the summer, but Orville could not help but mention some of their accomplishments over the winter and spring. He wrote,

> During the time the engine was building we were engaged in some very heated discussions on the principles of screw propellers, to which we had access, so that we worked out a theory of our own on the subject, and soon discovered, as we usually do, that all propellers built heretofore are *all wrong,* and then built a pair of propellers 8 $\frac{1}{8}$ ft. in diameter based on our theory, which are *all right!* (till we have a chance to test them down at Kitty Hawk and find out differently.) Isn't it astonishing that all these secrets have been preserved for so many years just so that we could discover them!! Well, our propellers are so different from any that have been used

before that they will have to either be a good deal better, or a good deal worse.

He ended the letter with a word of caution: "P.S.: Please do not mention the fact of our building a powered machine to anybody. The newspapers would take great delight in following us in order to record our *troubles*."

Orville had a good reason for including this warning. The Wright brothers were not the only ones trying hard to be the first to experience manned, powered flight.

Family matters prevented Orville and Wilbur from leaving for the Outer Banks of North Carolina in early summer. Their father, now seventy-five years old, was in the midst of a controversy with his denomination. It seemed that the denomination's treasurer had been embezzling church funds, and instead of allowing him to resign quietly, Bishop Wright had demanded a public apology from the man. When this was not forthcoming, the bishop went to the police, hoping to press criminal charges. This did not sit well with the United Brethren in Christ, who accused Milton Wright of making a public spectacle of a private church matter. Still, Bishop Wright clung firmly to his position and refused to be quieted.

The whole matter was going to come to a head at the denomination's conference in August 1903. Wilbur, who had helped his father write several articles about the situation, felt that he should go to the White River Conference with his father to show support. Orville agreed. Their father needed help, and they would not let him down. So Wilbur went off to the conference with his father while Orville continued with the finishing touches to the Flyer.

Things did not go well for Bishop Wright at the conference. By a vote of twenty-two to two, the denomination's leaders expelled Milton Wright from the United Brethren in Christ. It was a bitter blow to the entire family, and it was nearly a month before Wilbur and Orville felt that they could leave their dejected father.

During the first week of September, Orville and Wilbur disassembled the Flyer and packed it, along with tools, spare parts, a supply of canned food, various items of kitchenware, mosquito netting, new burlap for their beds, and a more than ample supply of blankets, into crates. The crates were then freighted by rail to Elizabeth City, North Carolina, where they would be shipped on to the camp at Kill Devil Hills.

Finally, on September 23, 1903, the Wright brothers themselves left Dayton for the Outer Banks. When they reached Elizabeth City, they received some unsettling news. The freight depot had burned to the ground several days before. As far as Orville and Wilbur knew, the Flyer, along with the rest of their shipment, may well have gone up in smoke, and no one who had worked at the freight depot could assure them that it had not. The brothers could do nothing about the situation but catch a boat to the Outer Banks, get to their campsite, and hope that their precious cargo had not been in the freight depot at the time of the fire.

When they finally reached their campsite at Kill Devil Hills, Orville and Wilbur were relieved to find that most of the crates they shipped ahead had already been delivered there, having passed through the freight depot before it burned down. And they were put totally at ease when they learned that the crates containing the Flyer were still en route from Dayton and would be arriving any day.

The old, wooden hangar was still standing, with the previous year's glider inside. The shed had been shifted several feet off its foundation by the wind, but it was still solid enough to serve as the men's new living quarters for the next two months or more, and Wilbur and Orville began referring to it as "the summer house." To house the Flyer, Orville and Wilbur needed to build a larger hangar, and as he had with the previous hangar, Orville had ordered ahead the lumber cut to size and had it delivered to the island.

Wilbur and Orville hired Bill Tate's brother Dan to help them build the new hangar. But as they worked away constructing the building, the weather, which was perfect gliding weather, proved too tempting for Orville and Wilbur. The brothers stopped building and got out the old glider. They lugged it to the top of the sand dune and took turns gliding. Orville was glad to see that his flying skills had not withered in the intervening months. In fact, these glides were more exhilarating than those of the year before. This was mostly due to the perfect wind they were experiencing, which caused the glider to almost hover for long periods without covering much distance on the ground.

Once the new hangar was built and repairs made to the old one, Wilbur and Orville continued to hone their flying skills, using the old glider while they waited for all the parts of the Flyer to arrive. But as the days rolled by, Wilbur seemed to be getting a little uneasy. Orville thought he knew why— Samuel Pierpont Langley.

Since the successful flight of his Aerodrome No. 5 in 1896, Langley had secured fifty thousand dollars in funding from the U.S. War Department to build and fly a full-sized version of his model, which he was calling the Great Aerodrome. It had taken over six years, but Langley and his crew were ready to test their flying machine any day now. Both Orville and Wilbur had doubts about the airworthiness of Langley's Great Aerodrome, but what if it flew? What would that mean for Orville and Wilbur? Only time would tell.

Finally, on October 9, the remainder of the parts of the Flyer arrived at Kill Devil Hills, and Orville and Wilbur got to work assembling them. They were still busy at work building their flying machine when George Spratt arrived at Kill Devil Hills to visit. Orville noted that George seemed to be impressed with their progress so far and the design of the Flyer, though he wondered whether the engine would be powerful enough to get the craft off the ground.

George had made it to the Outer Banks just as the weather turned cold, so cold, in fact, that he and Orville turned an old, used carbide can into a fireplace to try to warm their living quarters. The first time they lit a fire in the new fireplace, the fire filled the room with thick smoke. The next day they added a chimney to the improvised fireplace and funneled the smoke outside. This worked perfectly, keeping the inside of the living quarters warm. But at night when they climbed up to their beds, Wilbur began classifying the nights by the number of blankets he had to pile on top of him to keep warm. There were five-blanket nights, five-blankets-and-two-quilts nights, and five-blankets-and-two-quilts-plus-a-jug-of-hot-water nights.

By November 5, Orville and Wilbur had finished assembling the Flyer. The engine was in place, mounted on the bottom wing beside the pilot. The last thing to be attached was the chain-drive mechanism that ran from the engine to sprockets on one end of the propeller shafts. On the other end of the shafts, facing toward the back of the craft, were mounted the propeller blades that Orville and Wilbur had painstakingly fashioned. As they tightened the propellers and sprockets to the ends of the two shafts, Wilbur and Orville had a hard job getting them as tight as they thought they should be. But finally they managed to tighten them to a tension they thought would be okay.

Now it was time for a ground test of the craft. The first thing they did was fire up the engine. The engine sprang to life, but it would not run smoothly, and every so often it would cough and splutter. Finally the brothers tracked down the problem to the magneto. But before they could fix the problem, disaster struck. The chain-drive system was designed to work turning the propeller shaft at a constant torque. But each misfire of the engine caused the chain to jerk. The stress of these jerks was too great for the propeller shafts to bear, and the shafts broke loose from their mountings, twisting in the process.

Orville stood dumbfounded, looking at the twisted propeller shafts. He and Wilbur had brought lots of tools with them, but they had no tools suitable for repairing the shafts, and no machine shop was anywhere nearby.

"The only thing we can do is remove the shafts and send them back to Charlie in Dayton for repairs," Orville said gloomily.

Wilbur nodded.

That afternoon George decided to leave camp at Kill Devil Hills, and he agreed to take the twisted propeller shafts with him to Elizabeth City, where he would ship them off to Dayton.

In the meantime, while they waited for the repaired shafts to return, Orville and Wilbur managed to get the engine running smoother. They also continued to practice their flying skills on the old glider, but the wait was frustrating. However, the mail from home brought some good news that cheered them. One of Orville's friends had sent a newspaper, the front page of which carried the story of Langley's disastrous attempt to fly his Great Aerodrome on October 7, 1903. Orville read the article aloud to Wilbur. The Great Aerodrome, with Langley's assistant, Charles Manly, behind the controls, had been catapulted off the top of a houseboat on the Potomac River and immediately nose-dived into the river. The ungainly flying machine had been recovered from the water, and the article reported that Langley hoped to make another attempt to fly the Great Aerodrome in the future.

Orville watched as the news seemed to cheer his older brother. "We are in with a shot now to be first," he declared. "Winter is approaching, and Langley will not make another attempt to fly until the spring."

While the brothers waited for the repaired propeller shafts to return, Octave Chanute paid them a visit. He too was impressed with the design of the Flyer. But like George Spratt, he had doubts about the power of the engine. And such comments, coming from an esteemed engineer got Orville and Wilbur a little concerned. Had they miscalculated? According to their own calculations, they had not. But now they wondered whether they were wrong about how much power the engine needed to produce to fly the Flyer.

Chanute stayed only a few days at the Kill Devil Hills camp. It was bitter cold, too cold to be outside on the glider practicing, so the three men had sat around the fire most of the time talking.

"Where are those shafts, Orv?" Wilbur worried out loud one day after Chanute had left. "They should be here by now."

"Yes, they should," Orville replied. "I know that Charlie would have gotten right on to the job as soon as he received them. They'll be here any day now."

Ever since he had received a letter from Chanute the day before, Wilbur had been agitated. And Orville was feeling that way too, with good reason. The letter had contained a small article that Chanute had clipped from the newspaper stating that Samuel Langley and his team had recovered and repaired the Great Aerodrome and were planning to attempt to fly it again in early December.

Finally, on November 20 the repaired propeller shafts arrived at the Kill Devil Hills camp. Both brothers were dismayed to learn that although Charles had indeed gotten right onto the job, working around the clock to fix the shafts and get them on their way back to Orville and Wilbur as fast as possible, when the repaired shafts reached Elizabeth City, they had lain in the rebuilt freight depot for ten days awaiting shipment to Kitty Hawk.

Still, the brothers had the propeller shafts now, and if they hurried to install them and do some more ground tests, they figured that they had a good chance of getting the Flyer into the air ahead of Samuel Langley and his team.

Chapter 11

Success

I can't believe it!" Orville wailed as he looked at one of the repaired propeller shafts. He and Wilbur had fitted the shafts to the Flyer and tried them out twice with the engine running. The shafts worked fine, though Orville and Wilbur had to use some "Arnstein's," a tough adhesive they often used at the bicycle shop, to secure the sprockets to the end of the propeller shafts as tightly as they needed to be. But now as Orville peered at one of the repaired shafts, he noticed that it had a crack down its entire length. "We're going to need a new shaft. Maybe Charlie did something wrong when he originally made them. They just don't seem strong enough."

"But what could he have done wrong? The design is simple and straightforward," Wilbur said.

Wilbur's comment hung in the air. It was November 28, 1903, and snow flurries swirled around the camp at Kill Devil Hills. Both Orville and Wilbur knew that time was running out. Not only was winter arriving and it was bitter cold, but also Samuel Pierpont Langley was going to make another attempt soon to get his Great Aerodrome into the air. But how soon? That was the question that haunted Orville and Wilbur, who had not worked this hard to be the "runners up" in the quest to fly a manned, heavier-than-air flying machine. But they could not get the Flyer into the air with a cracked propeller shaft.

"One of us is going to have to go back to Dayton and help Charlie make two new shafts. The design might be simple and straightforward, but there's something wrong with it. The shafts have given out twice now," Orville said, digging his hands into his pockets to keep them warm. "We have to abandon the idea of a hollow shaft and make them from solid, high-grade steel. I know they'll be heavier than the hollow shafts, but they'll be stronger too."

Wilbur nodded in agreement. "I'll stay here and keep things going. We need more firewood split. You'd better get on your way first thing in the morning. It looks like another storm is coming."

The following morning Orville set out for Dayton with the old propeller shafts. Back at home Bishop Wright was jubilant because he had just sold a 320-acre farm he owned in Iowa and divided the proceeds among his four sons. If Orville and Wilbur wished, the $4,900 portion that was to go to them would be enough to keep them as they worked on the design of their flying machine. Orville was a little daunted by the gift and could not help wondering how he would feel if he spent all his money on flying machines and had nothing to show for it in the end.

At the bicycle shop Charlie and Orville set right to work fashioning new, solid steel propeller shafts. When they were finished and Orville had satisfied himself that the shafts were up to the task, it was time to get back to camp at Kill Devil Hills.

It was Wednesday, December 9, and Orville anticipated another boring train ride back to Elizabeth City, North Carolina, with the new propeller shafts stowed safely in the boxcar. Since he had traveled back and forth on this route eight times in the past three years, he took a couple of newspapers to read to pass the times on the train. As the train chugged off on its way east, he spread a copy of the *New York Times* out before him. Suddenly a headline in the paper caught his attention. "Hopes Dashed in Potomac," the headline read. Orville's heart quickened as he continued to read on. It was an account of Langley's latest attempt to fly. "On the signal to start the airplane glided smoothly along the launching tramway, until the end of the slide was reached. Then, left to itself, the aeroplane broke into two and turned completely over." The article went on to describe how the Great Aerodrome had sunk to the bottom of the Potomac River and how the pilot, Charles Manly, had narrowly escaped from the wreckage. Samuel Langley, who was watching from the deck of a nearby barge, was reported to be crestfallen at the disastrous event.

Orville could not help feeling a little sorry for Langley, especially when he saw some of the scathing cartoons depicting the crash and read an editorial demanding that the House of Representatives stop all payments for flying experiments. Orville doubted that Langley would ever attempt to fly again.

When Orville had finished reading the newspaper he folded it neatly away, glad that he would have some good news to tell Wilbur. After stowing the newspaper away, Orville got out a pencil and paper. Professor Langley, Secretary of the Smithsonian Institution, had spent over six years and $73,000 trying to achieve human, heavier-than-air flight. On the sheet of paper Orville began to tally up what he and Wilbur had spent so far trying to get the Flyer into the air. Two sets of propeller shafts, the train tickets, the supplies they had brought with them to Kill Devil Hills, the wood and fabric to build the craft, the casting of the engine block, and paying Dan Tate to help them build the new hangar. In all it came to less than $1,000.

As the train rumbled along, Orville sat and smiled with satisfaction. He and Wilbur both had only high school educations and limited funds, but now they were hopeful that they would become the first people ever to fly a manned, heavier-than-air-machine. Orville recognized that if they succeeded, it would be because of their approach—careful observation that produced useful and accurate data, sound scientific experiments, and determination and ingenuity. It was not about money or title or position.

Orville spent the rest of the trip thinking about refitting the new propeller shafts and preparing to fly. He hoped that the weather would hold, since they now had just ten days to accomplish their goal, having promised to be home in Dayton for Christmas.

When he arrived back at camp at Kill Devil Hills, Orville pulled out the newspaper and handed it to Wilbur. "Here, read this," he said, pointing to the article on Langley's mishap with the Great Aerodrome. "I think this will cheer you up."

Orville watched as a look of delight spread across his brother's face as he read.

"The prize is ours for the taking," Wilbur said to Orville when he had read the article.

The two brothers got straight to work fitting the two new propeller shafts and getting the Flyer ready to fly. Before the old shaft had cracked, Wilbur and Orville had been able to set their minds at ease. The output of the engine provided more than ample power to get and keep the Flyer aloft, even though the craft now weighed in at over 700 pounds and not the 625 pounds that had initially been anticipated.

With the Flyer ready to take to the air, Orville and Wilbur waited anxiously for the right weather conditions. The first sunny day was December 13. The wind was blowing at about fifteen miles per hour, and it was a perfect day for flying. There was just one problem: it was a Sunday, and the brothers would not break their word to their father and fly on the Sabbath—even if it might be the last chance they had to try.

Monday also dawned bright and sunny, and by lunchtime the brothers were ready to try the Flyer. They raised a flag on a nearby sand hill to signal the men at Kill Devil lifesaving station that they were going to attempt a flight. With the Flyer being so heavy, Orville and Wilbur had conscripted the help of the men at the lifesaving station to move the machine to its starting point. The flag was the pre-arranged signal that help was needed. The men would also serve as reliable witnesses in case the Flyer did make history.

The Flyer had no wheels, just skids for making a landing on the sand. For takeoff Orville and Wilbur had devised a sixty-foot-long rail made of two-by-fours. A dolly with wheels was placed on the rail, and the Flyer was placed on top of the dolly so that it could lift off freely into flight as the dolly ran along the rail. For their first attempt the brothers decided to set up the rail on the gently sloping side of a sand dune.

Forty-five minutes after the men from the life-saving station arrived, everything was ready for the attempt. The rail was laid, and the Flyer sat on the dolly at the top of it. Wilbur and Orville had agreed beforehand that they would flip a coin to see who got to make the first flight in the Flyer. Wilbur won the toss and got himself ready for the attempt. Once he was at the controls in the prone position on the bottom wing, the engine, which was mounted right beside him, was started. The propellers began to spin, and Wilbur was ready to fly. When he was ready to begin his run down the rail, he slipped off the wire that held the dolly and flying machine in place, and he was off.

The Flyer accelerated rapidly down the rail, and about four feet from the end, it lifted into the air. As it did so, Orville clicked his stopwatch to time the flight. But the craft did not stay in the air long. It climbed to a height of about fifteen feet and then quickly lost speed. Orville could see his brother move the double elevators at the front of the Flyer to bring the nose down, but as the nose came down, the tip of the left wing touched the ground. The Flyer spun around and came down heavily on its skids, breaking one of them. The whole flight had lasted just three and a half seconds, and the Wright brothers agreed that it was too short a duration to call it an actual flight. And besides, the craft had taken off from a downhill incline. Because of this there might be those who would say the Flyer actually glided rather than flew under its own power.

The men from the lifesaving station helped lug the Flyer back to its hangar, where Wilbur and Orville set to repairing it. The brothers were ready to make another attempt at flying on Thursday, December 17. It was a bitter cold day, ice had formed on the puddles around the area, and a north wind beat against the hangar. It was not ideal flying weather, but time was short, and Wilbur and Orville needed to make another attempt to fly before they had to return to Dayton for Christmas.

Once again the men from the lifesaving station helped get the Flyer to the end of the launch rail, which this time had been set up on the flat beach a short distance from their camp.

When everything was ready, Orville set up his camera on a tripod and aimed it at a point where he thought the Flyer would be airborne. He then enlisted one of the lifesavers, John Daniels, to snap a picture of the machine in flight. Little did Orville or John know that this photo would become one of the most reproduced images of the twentieth century.

The men started the engine of the Flyer and let it run for a few minutes to warm up before Orville climbed aboard to try his hand at flying the craft. Once his hips were settled snuggly into the wing-warping control cradle and one of his hands was on the elevator control lever, he reached down with his other hand and released the restraining wire that held the machine in place. The Flyer set off down the launch rail under its own power, with Wilbur running alongside to steady the right wing. At 10:35 AM, after covering forty feet of the rail, the Flyer lifted into the air. As it did so, John snapped the shutter of the camera and photographed the scene.

Orville scarcely had time to enjoy the sensation. The twin front elevators were oversensitive, making it too easy to overcorrect and causing the Flyer to dip and climb as it flew along. After twelve seconds in the air, the craft settled gently onto the sand for a landing, having covered a distance of 120 feet. This was long enough to qualify as a bona fide flight. Orville was jubilant. He and Wilbur had made history, and they knew it! Orville wrote of the experience that it was "the first time in the history of the world in which a machine carrying a man had raised itself by its own power into the air in full flight, had sailed forward without reduction of speed, and had finally landed at a point as high as that from which it had started."

After Orville's flight the Flyer was carried back to the head of the launch rail and placed on the dolly. By now everyone was cold, and the men all retreated inside the hangar to warm up. Half an hour later they emerged, ready for Wilbur to take another flight. This time the Flyer managed to stay aloft again for about twelve seconds, covering a distance of 175 feet in that time. Twenty minutes later the Flyer was turned around and ready for Orville to make another flight. This time Orville covered 200 feet in fifteen seconds. And then Wilbur took another turn behind the controls. This fourth flight was the longest of the day. Wilbur managed to stay in the air for fifty-nine seconds and covered an astonishing distance of 852 feet.

The men from the lifesaving station all pitched in to carry the Flyer back to its starting point at the head of the launch rail so that Orville could try flying it once again. This time Orville felt that he could control the craft well enough to coax it all the way down the beach, perhaps even as far as the lifesaving station. However, as Orville and Wilbur paused to catch their breath for a few moments, a gust of wind caught one of the Flyer's wingtips and flung the machine into the air.

Orville spun around and watched in horror as John jumped up and grabbed one of the wing struts. But the wind was too strong, and instead of holding the Flyer down, John was pulled into the air with it and dragged along. When the Flyer finally crashed to the ground, the engine broke loose and rolled onto John. Everyone ran to the site of the crash where John was screaming for help to get out of the wreckage. When the engine was finally pulled off him, John stood up, uninjured except for a few bumps and grazes.

Despite the fact that the Flyer was badly damaged, Orville was ecstatic. He and Wilbur had proved that man could fly. It was time to share the wonderful news with their family.

After the damaged Flyer had been stowed away in the hangar, and after they had eaten lunch, Orville and Wilbur walked to Kitty Hawk to send off a telegram to their father and Katharine. The Weather Bureau at Kitty Hawk was the only place on the island from which a telegram could be sent, and by the time they arrived there, Orville had composed the most significant message of his life:

Success four flights Thursday morning # all against twenty one mile wind started from Level with engine power alone # average speed through air thirty one miles longest 57 [sic] seconds inform Press home for Christmas. Orville Wright.

The telegraph operator in Norfolk, Virginia, who had to relay the telegram on to Dayton, sent a message back to Kitty Hawk, asking if he could share the news with a reporter friend of his. Orville and Wilbur sent back an emphatic one-word answer—"No." They trusted their father and sister to get the word out to the right people first.

Happily, Wilbur and Orville strolled back to their camp at Kill Devil Hills. It was time to pack up and head back to Dayton for Christmas.

Chapter 12

Huffman's Prairie

O rville stared at a stack of newspapers inside the train station in Elizabeth City. A headline caught his attention, and his heart sank as he started to read it aloud to Wilbur.

FLYING MACHINE SOARS 3 MILES IN TEETH OF HIGH WIND OVER SANDHILLS AND WAVES AT KITTY HAWK ON CAROLINA COAST

NO BALLOON ATTACHED TO AID IT

Three Years of Hard, Secret Work by Two Ohio Brothers Crowned with Success

ACCOMPLISHED WHAT LANGLEY FAILED AT

With Man as Passenger Huge Machine Flew Like Bird Under Perfect Control

BOX KITE PRINCIPLE WITH TWO PROPELLERS

The problem of aerial navigation without the use of a balloon has been solved at last.

Over the sand hills of the North Carolina coast yesterday, near Kitty Hawk, two Ohio men proved that they could soar through the air in a flying machine of their own construction, with the power to steer it and speed it at will.

Like a monster bird the invention hovered above the breakers and circled over the rolling sand hills at the command of the navigator and, after soaring for three miles, it gracefully descended to earth again and rested lightly upon the spot selected by the man in the car as a suitable landing place.

While the United States government has been spending thousands of dollars in an effort to make practicable the ideas of Professor Langley, of the Smithsonian Institute, Wilbur and Orville Wright, two brothers, natives of Dayton, O., have quietly, even secretly, perfected their invention, and put it to a successful test.

They are not yet ready that the world should know the methods they have adopted in conquering the air, but the Virginian-Pilot is able to state authentically the nature of their invention, its principle and its chief dimensions.

Orville and Wilbur sat glumly, lost in their thoughts. Orville could feel the veins in his neck pulsing against his stiff white collar. How dare they make up such rubbish? He wondered how the newspaper could have learned of their flight anyway.

"It must have been the person in the telegraph office in Norfolk," Wilbur said, answering the question Orville had not yet asked out loud.

"He sure has some imagination. And there's more too," Orville said.

Orville read on about how their flying machine had two propellers, one underneath to push it off the ground and one on the front to move it forward. The reporter also declared that it had climbed to sixty feet in the air and covered three miles over the surf.

"I wonder what will happen next? Nothing would surprise me," Orville said when he had finished reading.

"No," Wilbur agreed. "I don't doubt that some newspaper will report that we flew the Flyer home to Dayton to save time."

Orville chuckled. At least the two of them knew the truth.

Both brothers were glad when they finally made it home to Dayton. They had been gone for three months, and although summers had been hard to endure on the Outer Banks of North Carolina, Orville and Wilbur decided that the winter cold there had been much more challenging.

On their arrival home, Carrie, the family's housekeeper, made the brothers a delicious meal of porterhouse steak and their favorite desserts. Orville thought it was the best meal he had ever eaten.

Christmas 1903 was a very happy time as the extended Wright family all gathered to hear tales of Orville and Wilbur's flying adventures.

After New Year, it was time to start work on a new flying machine. Orville and Wilbur had brought the Flyer home with them in crates, but they decided against rebuilding it. As usual they had many ideas on how to make a new and improved flying machine.

Before they set to work designing and building a new Flyer, Wilbur and Orville decided to do what they could to counteract the crazy stories about them in the newspapers. They sat down and crafted a press release:

> It had not been our intention to make any detailed public statement concerning the private trials of our power "Flyer" on the 17th of December last; but since the contents of a private telegram, announcing to our folks at home the success of our trials, was dishonestly communicated to the newspapermen at the Norfolk office, and led to the imposition upon the public, by persons who never saw the "Flyer" or its flights, of a fictitious story incorrect in almost every detail, and since this story together with several pretended interviews or statements, which were fakes pure and simple, have been very widely disseminated, we feel impelled to make some corrections.

The brothers then wrote a simple, modest account of the four flights they had completed and ended with the statement,

> From the beginning we have employed entirely new principles of control; and as all

the experiments have been conducted at our own expense without assistance from any individual or institution, we do not feel ready at present to give out any pictures or detailed description of the machine.

Much to Orville and Wilbur's frustration, newspapers around the country printed the article but omitted the first paragraph that pointed out how the misinformation had become public in the first place.

Both brothers resigned themselves to an ongoing struggle with the press and continued with their flying plans. They had now reached the stage where they had the money and the time to work full-time on a new flying machine. They also realized that they needed to be close to Charles Taylor and the machine tools at the bicycle shop. The unanticipated trip back to Dayton with the broken propeller shafts had taught them this lesson. So Orville and Wilbur began looking for a place closer to home to fly their new machine. Eventually they settled on a rectangle of land owned by Torrance Huffman, president of the Fourth National Bank in Dayton. The land, called Huffman's Prairie, was one of the few remaining patches of uncultivated prairie in western Ohio and was flat and treeless. Huffman agreed to let the Wright brothers use his land as long as they were careful to move his grazing cows and horses first.

Orville and Wilbur were delighted and went straight to work building a shed to house their new Flyer at Huffman's Prairie. This new machine would be a little heavier and sturdier than their 1903 model. The brothers worked hard on the project with the help of Charles, and before the end of May, the new Flyer was ready to test.

One of the drawbacks of Huffman's Prairie was that two thoroughfares ran along its boundaries: the interurban railway line and the main Dayton-Springfield road. Although Orville and Wilbur tried hard not to let anyone know what they were doing, it was impossible to keep it a secret. They decided to counteract this by giving members of the press a limited idea of what they were up to. They announced a public display of flying in the new 1904 model Flyer. They asked only two things: first, that no photographs be taken, and second, that the press write an accurate and not an overinflated version of what they were about to see.

Orville and Wilbur need not have worried. Their "flying display" was an abysmal failure. There was too much wind, the new engine ran roughly, and the Flyer managed to fly only about 30 feet at head-height. No one was very impressed, and no sensational stories were written in the newspapers. What did happen was that reporters grew tired of watching the modest flights and concluded that it would be many years before Wilbur or Orville produced anything truly amazing, if indeed they ever did. This suited the Wright brothers just fine!

The brothers continued making improvements to their new Flyer, trying to improve its performance in the air. However, part of the problem with its performance in the air was the wind speed at

Huffman's Prairie. At Kill Devil Hills the year before, the brothers had launched the Flyer in winds of twenty miles per hour or above. But the wind at Huffman's Prairie was usually less than half that, and many days the wind was calm. This made it almost impossible some days for the new Flyer to get off the ground under its own power. Finally Orville and Wilbur came up with a solution to the problem—a catapult. They built a pyramidal structure about twenty feet tall, using four large poles braced with some cross timbers. At the apex of the pyramid was a pulley, over which ran a strong rope. To one end of the rope was attached six hundred pounds of metal weight. The other end of the rope ran around a series of pulleys that fed it under the length of the sixty-foot-long launch rail to the far end and then back along the top of the rail to the Flyer. Now, when the Flyer was ready for takeoff with its engine running and propellers spinning, the metal weight was released, pulling the rope down with it and hurtling the Flyer down the launch rail much faster than it could go under its own power. Before the flying season was over, Orville and Wilbur had increased the weight to eight hundred pounds.

The device worked perfectly. The first time he flew the Flyer using the catapult to launch him, Wilbur was able to cover two thousand feet. He continued to improve on the distance with subsequent flights. He told Orville that now he felt confident to try warping the wings and making a turn while in flight. And that is just what he did. He warped the wings of the Flyer, sending it into a banking half-circle turn, and landed facing in the direction opposite from which he had taken off. It was the first successful controlled turn of a powered aircraft in flight.

One day in September 1904 an elderly man drove up to the Wright house on Hawthorn Street in an Oldsmobile Runabout car. He introduced himself as Amos Root from Medina, Ohio, near Cleveland, and asked to talk with Wilbur and Orville. He explained that he had read an article about their experiments at Kitty Hawk the year before and had come to see the flying machine for himself.

There was something disarmingly straightforward about Amos, and both brothers took an immediate liking to him. They liked Amos even more when he explained to them that he had been the first man in Ohio to own a bicycle and had had a lifelong fascination with machinery. Amos said that he wrote and published a small biweekly newsletter entitled *Gleanings in Bee Culture.* He had started the newsletter as a way for him to pass on his expertise as a beekeeper, but the publication had grown to incorporate articles on all sorts of topics that interested him. Amos asked Wilbur and Orville if he could write an article about them for the newsletter. The brothers agreed to let him do this as long as he waited until winter, when their flying season would be finished, to publish it. Then, with a handshake, they invited Amos to come and see what they were working on.

On September 20, 1904, Amos drove Wilbur, Orville, and Charles out to Huffman's Prairie. When they arrived, Orville and Wilbur showed their guest the Flyer. Amos seemed very impressed by what he saw, and he asked countless questions about how the Flyer was put together and how they controlled it in the air. The kinds of questions he asked assured Orville that the man had not only a fascination with machinery but also a deep understanding of how and why it worked.

Finally the brothers rolled the Flyer out of the hangar and mounted it on the dolly on the launch rail. The catapult weight was hoisted and Wilbur started the Flyer's engine before climbing aboard the craft. When the weight was let go, the Flyer surged into the air, much to Amos's delight. Once in the air, Wilbur gained height, and then he banked the Flyer into a turn. He kept turning until he had flown in a complete circle over Huffman's Prairie before landing. On the ground Orville explaining that this was the first time that Wilbur had attempted such a turn. Amos was almost lost for words; he seemed scarcely able to believe what he was seeing. He told Orville that the flying display was far more than he had expected.

After Amos had left Dayton for home, Orville and Wilbur continued with their flying experiments, making longer and longer flights. On Tuesday, November 8, 1904, they were so pleased to learn that Teddy Roosevelt had won his first full term as President of the United States that they decided to take the Flyer out for a "victory flight." Everything went well, and Wilbur was able to circle above Huffman's Prairie four times, covering a distance of about three miles, by far the longest flight they had ever made. A month later Orville was able to match the distance flown. But by then it was time to pack the flying machine away for winter.

With their flying over for the year, Orville and Wilbur wrote to Amos, giving him permission to publish his article in *Gleanings in Bee Culture* anytime he wanted to. The article appeared in the January 1, 1905, edition of the newsletter. As Orville read the article, he smiled to himself. He and Wilbur had not misplaced their trust in the curious old man from Medina, Ohio. The article began:

Dear Friends,

I have a wonderful story to tell you—a story that, in some respects, out rivals the Arabian Nights fables—a story, too, with a moral that I think many of the younger ones need, and perhaps some of the older ones too if they will heed it. God in his great mercy has permitted me to be, at least somewhat, instrumental in ushering in and introducing to the great wide world an invention that may outrank the electric cars, the automobiles, and all other methods of travel, and one which may fairly take a place beside the telephone and wireless telegraphy....

In our issue for September 1, I told you of two young men, two farmer's boys, who love machinery, down in the central part of Ohio. I am now going to tell you something of two other boys, a minister's boys, who love machinery, and who are interested in the modern developments of science and art. Their names are Orville and Wilbur Wright, of Dayton, Ohio....

I found them in a pasture lot of 87 acres, a little over half a mile long and nearly as broad. The few people who occasionally got a glimpse of the experiment evidently considered it only another Darius Green, but I recognized at once they were really scientific explorers who were serving the world in much the same way that Columbus did when he discovered America, and just the same way that Edison, Marconi, and a host of others have done all along through the ages.

In running an automobile or a bicycle you have to manage the steering only to the right and left; but an air-ship has to be steered up and down also. When I first saw the apparatus it persisted in going up and down like the waves of the sea. Sometimes it would dig its nose in the dirt, almost in spite of the engineer. After repeated experiments it was finally cured of its foolish tricks, and was made to go like a steady old horse. This work, mind you, was all new. Nobody living could give them any advice. It was like exploring a new and unknown domain. Shall I tell you how they cured it of bobbling up and down? Simply by loading its nose or front steering apparatus with cast iron. In my ignorance I thought the engine was not large enough; but when fifty pounds of iron was fastened to its "nose" (as I will persist in calling it), it came down to a tolerably straight line and carried the burden with ease. There was a reason for this that I can not explain here. Other experiments had to be made in turning from right to left; and, to make the matter short, it was my privilege, on the 20th day of September, 1904, to see the first successful trip on an air-ship, without a balloon to sustain it, that the world has ever made, that is, to turn the corners and come back to the starting point. During all of these experiments they have kept so near to soft marshy ground that a fall would be no serious accident, either to the machine or its occupant. In fact, so carefully have they managed, that, during these years of experimenting, nothing has happened to do any serious damage to the machine nor to give the boys more than what might be called a severe scratch.... When the engine is shut off, the apparatus glides to the ground very quietly, and alights on something much like a pair of light sled runners, sliding over the grassy surface perhaps a rod or more....

Everybody is ready to say, "Well, what use is it? What good will it do?" These are questions no man can answer as yet....

I have suggested before, friends, that the time may be near at hand when we shall not need to fuss with good roads nor railway tracks, bridges, etc., at such an enormous expense. With these machines we can bid adieu to all these things. God's free air, that extends all over the earth, and perhaps miles above us, is our training field. Rubber tires, and the price of rubber, are no longer "in it." The thousand and one parts of the automobile that go to make its construction, and to give it strength, can all be dispensed with. You can set your basket of eggs almost any where on the upper or lower deck [wings], they will not even rattle unless it be when they come to alight. There are hundreds of queer things coming to light in regard to this new method of travel; and I confess it is not clear to me, even yet, how that little aluminum engine, with four paddles [propellers], does the work....

The operator takes his place lying flat on his face. This position offers less resistance to the wind. The engine is started and got up to speed. The machine is held until ready to start by a sort of trap to be sprung when all is ready; then with a tremendous flapping and snapping of the four-cylinder engine, the huge machine springs aloft. When it first turned that circle and came near the starting point, I was right in front of it; and I said then, and I believe still, it was one of the grandest sights, if not the grandest sight, of my life. Imagine a locomotive without any wheels, we will say, but with white wings instead, we will further say—a locomotive made of aluminum. Well, now, imagine this white locomotive, with wings that spread 20 feet each way, coming right toward you with a tremendous flap of its propellers, and you will have something like what I saw....

When Columbus discovered America he did not know what the outcome would be, and no one at that time knew; and I doubt if the wildest enthusiast caught a glimpse of what really did come from his discovery. In a like manner these two brothers have probably not even a faint glimpse of what their discovery is going to bring to the children of men.

Nor did Orville and Wilbur have the faintest glimpse of the unbelievable changes that were about to occur in their own lives.

Chapter 13

Trying to Sell a Secret

Orville and Wilbur Wright both hoped that 1905 would be their best year ever. In the past year the Flyer had proved itself as a sturdy, controllable aeroplane. Now it was time to think about how best to make money from their invention.

On January 3 Wilbur visited local congressman and fellow Republican Robert Nevin. The congressman listened attentively to all Wilbur had to say and suggested that the brothers write up a proposal of how the Flyer would be useful to the United States War Department and under what conditions they would sell it to them.

When Orville heard of the positive response Wilbur had received from the congressman, his hopes rose. The brothers had set out on the right path after all. But it did not take long for things to become so complicated that they were difficult to follow. The problem revolved around the fact that Orville and Wilbur's attorney had not yet been able to secure any patents for them. Because of this the brothers refused to demonstrate their flying machine for anyone who might be interested in purchasing it, nor would they allow any photographs to be taken of it. This, along with the secrecy in which they had worked for the past five years, led many people to believe that the Wright brothers were confidence tricksters—two bicycle salesmen from Dayton, Ohio, who were trying to fool the government into thinking they actually had a working flying machine.

The situation was not easy to solve, and Wilbur and Orville were very stubborn about the point. They asked the War Department to sign up to buy their Flyer sight unseen. They did add clauses to the proposed contract that if, after the government had paid for it, the Flyer did not live up to their claims, they would refund the money to the War Department. But they received a letter back from the War Department informing them that it was still too risky a proposition, especially since the War Department was still smarting over Langley's spectacular waste of fifty thousand dollars of its money.

Feeling annoyed that their own government could not see the huge potential of their invention, Orville and Wilbur agreed to offer the Flyer for sale in England and France. They decided that whoever made the first offer could have the Flyer. However, no one in either country showed much immediate interest.

Frustrated with the commercial side of flying machines, Orville and Wilbur returned to what they knew best—tinkering with flying machines. They took the engine off the 1904 Flyer and burned the rest of the craft. They were ready to construct a new model and did not want anyone to see how the old Flyer had been put together. The new Flyer, with its better control system, was ready to fly in June. But by late August it lay in tatters. Just after his thirty-fourth birthday, Orville was flying the Flyer when it started to undulate in the air. He lost control of the craft, which crashed to the ground and rolled over. Orville emerged from the wreckage with only minor cuts and bruises. This was amazing, since the Flyer had plunged to the ground from thirty feet in the air and catapulted Orville through the top wing on impact.

Just four days after the accident, Orville read about an even more horrific crash. Daniel Maloney, a geometry teacher and flying enthusiast from California, had been lifted off the ground in a glider by a hot-air balloon, a feat that was billed as "The most daring feat ever accomplished by man." At a height of three thousand feet in the air, the glider was released from the balloon. It was supposed to glide gracefully back down to earth with Maloney in it in front of hundreds of spectators. But that is not what happened. Instead the glider plummeted to the ground in about seven seconds, killing Maloney and wrecking the glider. For Orville and Wilbur, as they went back to their own flying experiments in the repaired Flyer, hearing such a story was a reminder that flying was still very dangerous.

Throughout 1904 and now with their 1905 model Flyer, Orville and Wilbur had noted an intermittent

problem when the wing warping failed to respond
as it should and return the Flyer back to equilibrium in the air. During a flight on September 28, as
he was banking to the left in a turn, Orville noticed
that he was fast closing in on a honey locust tree.
To avoid a collision with the tree, he moved his hips
in the wing-warping control cradle to the right to
bring up the left wing and return the Flyer to a level
flying position. But when he moved his hips to the
right, nothing happened—the left wing did not rise,
and the craft did not return to equilibrium. In des-
peration, all Orville knew to do was turn the front
elevator to its extreme down position and hope that
he could get the Flyer onto the ground before it
crashed into the tree. To his surprise Orville noticed
that as soon as he did this, the left wing came up
and the Flyer regained its equilibrium, narrowly
missing the honey locust tree.

As Orville and Wilbur talked over what had just
happened, they soon came to the realization that
they had solved that last riddle of controlled flight.
When it was flying and making a tight turn, the
Flyer had to contend not only with its own weight in
the air but also with an extra load from the centrifugal force being exerted on it. This was taxing
the engine, already running at full power, so that it
could not maintain enough speed to keep the Flyer
in the air. As a result the wing that was angled down,
and was traveling slower than the wing angled up,
was effectively stalled and not producing enough
lift to respond to the control. But when the elevator
was put in the down position, as Orville had done,

gravity kicked in. As the front of the Flyer began to drop, it provided enough extra power to move the wing from the stall position and cause it to respond and lift back up to a level position. Once there, with no more centrifugal force on it, the engine could get the Flyer back up to speed.

Armed with this understanding, Orville had more confidence behind the controls of the Flyer than ever before. He took to the skies again, and the following Friday he circled above Huffman's Prairie fourteen times before running low on gas. He and Wilbur then fitted a larger, three-gallon fuel tank to the Flyer, and the next Tuesday Orville flew fifteen miles. Two days later Wilbur took over, and he covered twenty-four miles at an average speed of thirty-eight miles per hour.

Now, Wilbur and Orville decided, it was time to show their invention to a few well-chosen people so that they would have credible witnesses to what they were doing. They invited thirty prominent citizens from Dayton out to Huffman's Prairie. Each person had to sign a document saying that he would not reveal what he was about to see until the Wright brothers gave him permission to do so, and that he would not photograph the Flyer. Orville and Wilbur took pains to make sure that none of the invited guests were knowledgeable about engineering so that they would not be able to describe the Flyer to others in technical terms.

Orville took the controls of the Flyer while Wilbur controlled the crowd on the ground and took official photographs of the event. On the first flight, Orville

flew twelve miles around Huffman's Prairie in twenty-
one minutes. The following day the group reassem-
bled to see him cover ten miles in seventeen minutes
and then fifteen miles in twenty-six minutes. As the
last flight was completed, two interurban trolleys
rattled past on the railway line that bordered the
prairie, and many of the passengers aboard craned
their necks for a look at the strange sight.

With the successful completion of the demonstration, Orville and Wilbur had reliable witnesses
who could testify to their sustained flights and a set
of clear photographs of the event. To this evidence
Orville added a description of what it was like to fly:

The ground under you is at first a perfect
blur, but as you rise the objects become
clearer. At a height of one hundred feet you
feel hardly any motion at all, except for the
wind which strikes your face. If you do not
take the precaution to fasten your hat before
starting, you have probably lost it by this
time.

The operator moves a lever; the right wing
rises, and the machine swings about to the
left. You make a very short turn, yet you do
not feel the sensation of being thrown from
your seat, so often experienced in automobile and railway travel. You find yourself facing toward the point from which you started.
The objects on the ground now seem to be
moving at a much higher speed, though you
perceive no change in the pressure of the

wind on your face. You know then that you are traveling with the wind.

When you near the starting point, the operator stops the motor while still high in the air. The machine coasts down at an oblique angle to the ground, and after sliding fifty or a hundred feet comes to rest. Although the machine often lands at a speed of a mile a minute, you feel no shock whatever, and cannot, in fact, tell the exact moment at which it first touched the ground.

The motor close beside you kept up an almost deafening roar during the whole flight, yet in your excitement you did not notice it until it stopped!

After the demonstration, the Wright brothers dismantled the Flyer and stored it in a shed behind their house. Meanwhile they were still corresponding with representatives of the United States, British, and French governments about selling their invention. One way or another the problem always came down to the same thing: the Wright brothers were unwilling to show or demonstrate the Flyer to prospective buyers, and the governments would not buy it without their representative seeing the Flyer first.

Then Wilbur and Orville received some good news. The U.S. Patent Office granted them two patents, number 821 and number 393. These patents covered the wing-warping technique and the lateral control system. However, even with the patents in place, things moved slowly.

Then in October 1906 a Brazilian, Alberto Santos-Dumont, managed to fly two hundred feet. His demonstration had taken place in Paris, and according to the reports, the French had gone wild with excitement, exclaiming that Santos-Dumont had "conquered human flight."

When Wilbur and Orville read the accounts of the flight, they were not at all concerned about what the Brazilian had accomplished. And they were not concerned that the Europeans would catch on to their ideas anytime soon. They knew it was one thing to fly a machine for a short distance in a straight line low to the ground, but it was quite another thing to circle for mile after mile high above the earth.

Around this time a businessman named Charles Flint contacted Orville and Wilbur and asked them to visit him in New York City. Orville soon discovered that Flint was one of America's leading financiers of military equipment. Flint had purchased ships for the Japanese, Russian, and Brazilian governments. Wilbur and Orville's hopes rose: perhaps Charles Flint was the man to get things done for them at home and in Europe.

At a meeting in Manhattan on December 17, 1906, Flint offered to be the Wright brothers' business agent in Europe. He felt sure that he could interest a foreign country in buying their Flyer and patents. This was just the opportunity Wilbur and Orville were hoping for, and they signed a contract with Flint's company.

Now it was time for action. Flint explained that one of the brothers should go to France to meet with

his representative there. Just as they were deciding
who should go, Orville and Wilbur received a letter
from the United States War Department:

> I am directing the President of the Board to
> enclose copies of two letters referring to your
> aeroplane, for your information, and to say
> that the Board has before it several proposi-
> tions for the construction and test of aero-
> planes, and if you desire to take any action
> in the matter, will be glad to hear from you
> on the subject.

Suddenly things were moving forward on not
just one but two fronts. The brothers decided that
Wilbur should go to France while Orville stayed home
to negotiate an agreement with the United States
government.

Wilbur departed for Le Havre, France, in mid-
May 1907, and Orville rolled up his sleeves and got
to work on his end of things. The brothers had
already discussed asking $100,000 for a completed
Flyer. This was a large sum of money, but Orville
noted that the War Department had given Langley
$50,000, and Langley had not managed to produce
a viable flying machine with that amount. But as
letters went back and forth between Dayton and
Washington, D.C., Orville learned that the U.S.
Congress would have to approve the expenditure of
such a large amount, and Congress was not cur-
rently in session. Since Orville could do little more
until then, he turned his attention to tracking

Wilbur's progress in France. Each letter, which took about three weeks to arrive, told a different story. Sometimes it sounded as though Wilbur was only hours away from making a sale, and then the next letter would dash all hopes.

Finally Orville decided that there was only one thing to do. He and Charles Taylor would go to France and take along with them the Flyer they had just finished modifying. Orville was particularly proud of this new model. He had added a seat to it so that he would no longer have to lie down to fly, and had installed a more powerful engine to compensate for the extra drag that a man in an upright position would create.

Orville left first, arriving in Paris in mid-July, and Charles followed soon after with the crated Flyer. Once in Paris Orville soon realized what a difficult job Wilbur and the Flint Company representative had had in trying to deal with the French government. Summer turned into fall, and still there was no end of negotiations in sight. The Flyer continued to sit in a warehouse in its shipping crate, and by October 1907 Wilbur, Orville, and Charles had had enough. They returned home with little to show for five months of bargaining.

But better news awaited Orville and Wilbur in the United States. In their absence the U.S. War Department had decided to offer the Wright brothers a contract worth $25,000 for a flying machine. But because this was government business, it had one stipulation. The Army had to put out a notice to attract other bidders in the process. A copy of the bid was enclosed. It stated that the flying machine must be "supported entirely by the dynamic reaction of the atmosphere and having no gas bag," and it had to be "quickly and easily assembled and taken apart and packed for transportation in army wagons." The craft also had to have "a speed of at least forty miles per hour in still air." It also needed to carry a pilot and passenger and make a demonstration flight of "at least one hour during which time the flying machine must remain continuously in the air without landing. It shall return to the starting point and land without any damage that would prevent it immediately starting another flight. During this trial flight of one hour it must be steered in all directions without difficulty and at all times under perfect control and equilibrium."

Once Orville and Wilbur read this, they felt confident that they would be awarded the contract. There was no other flying machine in the world but theirs that could do those things. But everyone was taken by surprise when forty bids were submitted for the contract. Dreamers and cranks had submitted most of these. A prison inmate stated in his bid that he wanted $45 per pound for his nonexistent flying machine, and another man claimed in his bid that he could build a flying machine able to zoom through the air at five hundred miles per hour. In fact, once all the bids were sifted through, only two were credible: the Wright brothers' Flyer and a machine that Augustus Herring said he could build.

Herring had accompanied Octave Chanute to Kitty Hawk for a visit back in 1902. Although Orville and Wilbur were confident that he could not deliver an aeroplane per his bid, it was another reminder that secrecy was important. According to sources the brothers knew, Herring planned to use what he had observed at Kitty Hawk to compete against Orville and Wilbur.

The bid from Herring posed a problem because it was five thousand dollars lower than Orville and Wilbur's bid, and the War Department was obliged to accept it as the lowest bid. But since the department really wanted the Flyer, it accepted the Wright brothers' bid as well and commissioned both parties to deliver an aeroplane that met the specifications.

On February 10, 1908, the postman delivered a special letter to Orville and Wilbur:

> I am directed by the Chief Signal Officer of the Army to place an order with you for the articles listed below...
>
> ITEM:
>
> One (1) heavier-than-air flying machine, in accordance with Signal Corps Specification No. 486, dated December 23, 1907 at $25,000.

One month later the brothers received more good news. The Flint Company had managed to wrap up negotiations with the French, and a syndicate in France had agreed to purchase the Wright brothers' patents along with the right to manufacture, license, and sell the Wright aeroplanes in France.

Now Orville and Wilbur had not one but two contracts and two sets of demonstration flights to complete. But before that could happen, two things had to take place. First, they had to build a second Flyer for Orville to demonstrate, and second, they had to both become proficient at flying the aircraft from a sitting position using their latest control system. However, they also needed to keep the Flyer away from prying eyes until this was done. It was time to return to the Outer Banks of North Carolina one last time.

A Record-Setting Time

The plan came together quickly. Wilbur would go to the Outer Banks and prepare their old camp at Kill Devil Hills while Orville and Charles stayed behind in Dayton to build another Flyer. As soon as the craft was finished, they would crate it up and take it with them to join Wilbur. Now, more than ever, Orville and Wilbur felt pressured. Another distinguished man—none other than Alexander Graham Bell, the inventor of the telephone—had entered the race to conquer flight.

Bell had been interested in flight for over ten years, and in October 1907 he had assembled a team of four able young men to help him put a man in the air in a heavier-than-air craft. The four young men were Glenn Curtiss, a motorbike racer; Casey Baldwin and Douglas McCurdy, two recent graduates from the University of Toronto; and Thomas Selfridge, a West Point graduate. As it turned out, the fate of two of these men would be interwoven with the Wright brothers in the years to come. The group called themselves the Aerial Experiment Association (AEA), and at the same time that Orville was on his way to Kill Devil Hills they managed to fly an aeroplane one hundred feet. It was reported that their craft lacked controls, but with the veteran inventor Alexander Graham Bell on the case, no one doubted that the association would make rapid progress.

The last thing Orville and Wilbur needed was for the French syndicate or the United States Army to be won over by this new group. So for the first time ever, both brothers were willing to sacrifice slow, methodical progress for speed.

Orville had crated up the 1907 Flyer and taken it to France with him, though as things had turned out, it was never assembled and flown there. In fact, it was still crated up and sitting in a warehouse in France, and Wilbur would use that Flyer for flying demonstrations when he returned to Europe. Orville would use the new Flyer he and Charles were carrying with them to test at Kill Devil Hills.

Orville and Charles joined Wilbur at Kill Devil Hills on April 25, 1908. The two old sheds that had once formed their camp had fallen down, and some boys from Nags Head had carried away anything they found interesting at the old site. Bill Tate had died, and some of the old members of the Kill Devil Hills lifesaving station had moved on as well. Still,

Wilbur had things under control. A new shed had been built, and the brothers set to work assembling the Flyer and preparing to fly it.

Everything went smoothly except for the strange visitors who wandered into camp. These folks had a variety of excuses for coming. One said he was looking for a broken telegraph cable, another that he had signed up at the lifesaving station and wished to "meet the neighbors." However, both Wilbur and Orville were suspicious that news had leaked out about their trials. As a result, they refused to fly while any strangers were in camp, but they had no way to search the entire area. They had a hunch that reporters may well be in hiding in the dunes spying on them.

As it turned out, their hunch was confirmed by a series of articles and the first published photographs of the Flyer that began appearing in national newspapers and magazines. One reporter wrote:

> The machine rose obliquely into the air. At first it came directly toward us, so that we could not tell how fast it was going, except that it appeared to increase in size as it approached. In the excitement of this first flight, men trained to observe details under all sorts of distractions forgot their cameras, forgot their watches, forgot everything but this aerial monster chattering over our heads. As it neared us we could plainly see the operator in his seat working the upright levers close to his side. When it was almost

squarely over us there was a movement of
the forward and rear gliding planes, a slight
curving of the larger planes at one end and
the machine wheeled at an angle every bit as
gracefully as an eagle flying close to the
ground could have done.

When they heard of these accounts, Orville and
Wilbur realized that they could do nothing except
continue with their plans. Wilbur soon mastered the
new flight control system. The biggest change was in
the wing-warping controls. Since the pilot was now
sitting upright to fly, the hip cradle had been
replaced by two levers, one on either side of the pilot.
The levers operated the wing warping by being
either pulled back or pushed forward, depending
on which way the pilot wanted the Flyer to turn. In
fact, Wilbur was feeling so confident with the new
control system that on the morning of May 14 he
took the first passenger aloft. His passenger was
Charlie Furnas, a mechanic from Dayton who had
come to Kill Devil Hills to help Wilbur rebuild the
camp. The flight was a success.

Later in the day, Orville held the stopwatch while
Wilbur made another flight. Four, five, six, seven
minutes of flawless flying, and then the Flyer flew
behind a sand dune. Orville waited patiently for it
to reappear. Suddenly the noise of the propellers
stopped, and Orville could hear only the cries of the
gulls. Orville, Charles Taylor, and Charlie Furnas
sprinted across the sand and up the dune to see
what had happened. The Flyer was lying nose first

in the sand. Wilbur sat in a tangle of wires, but when he saw Orville, he waved. Fortunately he had only cuts and bruises as a result of the crash, but the Flyer had sustained a lot of damage. It would take weeks to repair it. This meant that there would be no more test flights on the Outer Banks. It was time for Wilbur to patch up his injuries and prepare to head for Europe, leaving the cause of the crash unknown.

The Wright brothers left Kill Devil Hills separately. Wilbur left the day after the accident, while Orville remained behind to pack up the damaged Flyer. He then returned home to Dayton via Washington, D.C.

It was only the second time that Orville and Wilbur had taken on separate tasks, and each man had enough work to do to keep five men busy. Back in Dayton, Orville rolled up his sleeves and set to work repairing the Flyer, overseeing the manufacture of five new sets of Flyer parts to be shipped to Wilbur as soon as possible, and writing a full account of their discoveries for the record. Although Orville did not enjoy writing for publication, he took this task very seriously, as it was one way to establish the breakthroughs in flying that the brothers had made as well as their right to hold the patents for them.

There were distractions too. It appeared to Orville that the country had gone mad over the stories and pictures that had been published during their short stint on the Outer Banks. As a result a constant parade of visitors was coming through the bicycle shop door, wanting to meet the brothers, and over five hundred letters had soon piled up waiting to be read and the important ones answered.

Wilbur wrote home to Orville from France nearly every day. Most of the news he reported was mixed. When the Flyer had been shipped to France the previous year, French customs officers had apparently pulled just about every piece of the craft out of its packing and then dumped all the pieces back into any old crate in a heap. Wilbur complained that sorting out the jumbled mess was going to delay his flying demonstration by up to a month. Then, on July 4, he was severely burned when a radiator hose ruptured, spraying his left arm and chest with boiling water. Despite the injury, Wilbur assured Orville, the flight demonstration was still moving forward.

Then, on August 8, 1908, much to Orville's delight, American newspaper headlines announced the sensational flight of Wilbur Wright in Le Mans, France. Orville read the accounts with riveted attention. The accounts reported that Wilbur had made two circuits in the Flyer, over a racecourse, each lasting a minute. The flight was enough to convince the French that the Americans were superior aviators. French scientists and flying enthusiasts fell all over themselves to apologize for doubting that the Wright brothers were telling the truth about their invention. One of the leading French authorities on flight said simply, "We are as children compared to the Wrights," while Louis Blériot, the most experienced French flyer, commented after seeing the way the Flyer banked and turned, "I consider that for us in France, and everywhere, a new era in mechanical flight has commenced. I am not sufficiently calm after the event to thoroughly express my opinion."

More flights followed, and over three thousand French people flocked to see the "miracle in the sky" for themselves. All of this was wonderful news to Orville, as he was in the final stages of preparing for his own demonstration flights for the army. These flights were to take place at Fort Myer, Virginia, near Washington, D.C., at the end of August.

Orville arrived at Fort Myer on August 20 and inspected the parade ground that would serve as the airfield for the army tests and demonstration flights. The parade ground was seven hundred feet wide and one thousand feet long and was located beside Arlington Cemetery. It was smaller than Orville would have liked, but it was suitable enough to continue with the demonstration.

The Flyer traveled very well in its crate, and Orville estimated that it would take five days to assemble, and then, weather permitting, the trial flights could begin. Finally, on the morning of September 3, 1908, Orville announced that he would attempt a flight that afternoon.

At 4:30 PM the Flyer was placed on the launch rail and made ready to fly. Charles Taylor and Charlie Furnas took their positions and spun the propellers to start the engine, which failed to start on the first try. Again the two Charlies spun the propellers, and this time the engine sputtered to life. Orville was seated behind the control. All was ready. The catapult weight was let go, and the Flyer surged down the rail and into the air. As the plane gained altitude, the crowd of about one thousand people who had gathered to see it fly let out a gasp of delight.

The Flyer reached the end of the field, and Orville banked it into a turn and flew over Arlington Cemetery. After one circuit of the airfield, at a height of about thirty-five feet, Orville began a second circuit. But during this circuit he made a mistake with the new control handles, which he was still getting used to. The Flyer immediately dropped in altitude, and Orville could see that he was on a collision course with a large tent set up at the parade ground. As quickly as he could, he shut off the engine and slammed the Flyer down onto the ground, where the craft abruptly stopped in a cloud of dust, doing some minor damage to the skids. But at least Orville had avoided hitting the tent. Frustrated with himself for the mistake he had made with the controls, Orville hoped to redeem himself on subsequent flights.

On the morning of September 9, with few spectators on hand, Orville took off in the Flyer again. This time he stayed aloft for fifty-seven and a half minutes, setting a new world record for flight duration. Later that day he made another flight, which lasted for sixty-two minutes. After this flight, as the daylight was fading, Orville took off yet again. This time he had a passenger, Lieutenant Frank Lahm, next to him. This flight lasted six minutes and set a new world record for the duration of a flight with a passenger.

Over the next several days, Orville continued to make record-breaking flights. He set a new altitude record, flying to a height of 200 feet, and then on a subsequent flight stretched the altitude record to 310 feet. And he broke his own duration record by staying aloft for one hour, fourteen minutes. In all, in just four days of flying, Orville managed to set nine world records. He was very pleased both with himself and with the performance of the Flyer.

Late in the afternoon of September 17, Orville decided to go up for another flight. This time he took with him another passenger, Lieutenant Thomas Selfridge. Although he was one of the members of Alexander Graham Bell's AEA team, Selfridge was also a member of the army board that needed to approve the final purchase of the Flyer after testing, and Orville felt obliged to take him aloft.

The two Charlies spun the propellers, and the engine rattled to life. The catapult weight was dropped, and soon the Flyer was aloft. Orville had made three circuits of the field at an altitude of about one hundred feet when he heard a strange tapping noise behind him. He turned quickly to see what it was but saw nothing out of the ordinary. Still, he decided to land the Flyer and check out the noise. But before he could do so, he heard two loud bangs behind him. Suddenly the Flyer began to shudder and vibrate. Thinking that one of the chains that drove the propellers had snapped, Orville quickly shut off the engine and prepared to glide the Flyer in for a landing. No sooner had he shut off the engine than the Flyer veered right toward Arlington Cemetery. Orville quickly pulled on the control levers to activate wing warping and adjust the rudder and bring the Flyer back under control. But when he did so, nothing happened.

Orville continued to pull frantically on the control levers, and to his relief the right wing lifted, and the Flyer began to turn in the opposite direction. Orville activated the wing warping in the opposite direction to bring the Flyer back to level and under control. But as he did so, the nose of the Flyer suddenly dropped until the craft was perpendicular to the ground.

"Oh! Oh!" Orville heard Selfridge utter as the Flyer began to fall out of control toward the ground. Orville tried to get the nose up by frantically moving the front elevator to its maximum "up" position. He thought that this was beginning to work. Yes, the nose was beginning to lift. But it was too late. Orville heard the crashing bang as dust burst around him. He felt a searing pain in his left thigh, and then everything went black.

Orville was carried from the crash site by stretcher and taken to the army hospital where the gashes on his face and head were treated, the badly broken bone in his left thigh was set and the leg put in traction, and several broken ribs were taped. He was still drifting in and out of consciousness when Katharine arrived to take over as his nursing assistant. Octave Chanute came to visit Orville in the hospital and told him that Thomas Selfridge had not survived very long after the flight. Selfridge had been operated on for his head injuries but had died soon afterward.

News of Selfridge's death was a bitter blow to Orville, who asked Charles Taylor to bring various parts of the Flyer to him in the hospital so that he could try to figure out what had gone wrong to cause the crash. Eventually Orville concluded that one of the propeller blades had cracked, causing a vibration that set off a chain of events that loosened the vertical rudder, causing the Flyer to swerve and dive. Orville drew some consolation from the fact that Lieutenant Selfridge had not been killed as the result of a mistake he had made at the controls of the Flyer but because of a mechanical failure. Still, it was disheartening to think that he was at the controls in the first crash to kill a flying-machine passenger.

Orville remained in the hospital for six weeks with his left leg in traction. During this time he followed Wilbur's amazing ride to fame in France. Four days after Orville's crash at Fort Myer, Wilbur had taken to the air and flown for an hour and a half, breaking Orville's recently set flight duration record.

Finally, in early November, Orville was well enough to return to Dayton in a wheelchair. Once home, either Katharine or Charles would wheel him each morning and afternoon to and from the workshop at the bicycle shop. But the pain in his back and leg did not allow Orville to stay long. Gradually, though, Orville's strength began to return, and by the time he was back on his feet, he was toying with the idea of heading to Europe to help Wilbur.

Katharine jumped at the opportunity and made all of the necessary travel arrangements, including arranging for housekeeper Carrie Kayler and her new husband, Charles Grumbach, to move into the house on Hawthorn Street to care for their father while they were gone.

Orville and Katharine set out for France on New Year's Day 1909. They were in particularly high spirits, as they had just learned the day before that Wilbur had won the 1908 Michelin Cup and a prize of twenty thousand francs for flying the greatest distance during that year. The record that had won Wilbur the prize was covering a distance of ninety miles in two hours, eighteen minutes. And the French government, in recognition of the Wright brothers' flying accomplishments, announced that Orville and Wilbur had been awarded the country's highest honor, the Legion of Honor.

When they arrived in Paris on January 12, 1909, Orville and Katharine found their brother's celebrity hard to grasp. The newspapers claimed that the French had taken to Wilbur Wright like no other American since Benjamin Franklin. Crowds clamored around Wilbur in the streets, and every word that he uttered was written down and printed somewhere. Still, the public and press always wanted more, and Orville looked forward to getting away from the public eye and traveling to Pau, a small country retreat where Wilbur was to undertake some test flights and train three young men to be pilots.

Regrettably Pau was a small country retreat only until the Wrights got there. After their arrival people from all over Europe came to see the amazing spectacle of the "MM. Wright fréres." King Alfonso XIII of Spain arrived with his camera in hand to watch Wilbur fly, and King Edward VII of England watched the demonstrations with American million-aire J. P. Morgan. In addition, King Victor Emmanuel III of Italy came to Pau to view the spectacle.

Everything that the Wright brothers did was reported or copied. Thousands of replicas of Wilbur's green flying cap were made, and when one female passenger tied her skirt at the bottom to stop it from flapping around in flight, the "hobble skirt" fashion was born.

Orville found all this attention tiring and mar-veled that Wilbur had been able to get anything done amid it all. Only Katharine appeared to really enjoy all the attention.

In May 1909 the Wright siblings set out for home via England, where they made arrangements with a London machine shop to manufacture "Wright Planes" for the British market. Then it was time to get back to the United States.

Orville, Wilbur, and Katharine arrived in New York Harbor on May 11 amid a flotilla of welcoming boats. Thousand of spectators lined the dock as the Wrights disembarked and were whisked off to a reception at the Waldorf Hotel. But all this was nothing compared to the welcome that awaited them in their hometown.

In Dayton ten thousand people were waiting around the train station to meet Orville, Wilbur, and Katharine, who were at the center of an all-day party. Orville longed for things to get back to nor-mal. He and Wilbur had Flyers to build and a second round of demonstrations and tests at Fort Myer,

Virginia, to prepare for. Despite his serious accident there, Orville wanted to return and complete the tests himself.

Chapter 15

Success and Sadness

O rville stood nervously on the platform, staring out at the group of prominent men and women gathered in the East Room of the White House. It was June 10, 1909, a month since he had arrived home from France, and so much had happened in that time. Orville tried hard to take in what President Taft was saying, but it was hard to concentrate on the speech while feeling so nervous. He did manage to hear the president talk about the Wright brothers' genius, hard work, perseverance, and, above all, modesty. This made Orville blush, and although he did not look at Wilbur, who was standing beside him, he knew that such praise would embarrass his brother as well.

President Taft concluded his speech with the hope that the invention of the aeroplane would lead to greater peace in the world and not become just a weapon of war. Then he added, "You made this discovery by a course that we of America like to feel is distinctly American—by keeping your nose right at the job until you had accomplished what you had determined to do." With the speech over, President Taft presented a boxed gold medal to both Wilbur and Orville and then ushered the brothers out onto the White House porch for a photo opportunity with reporters.

Unlike Orville and Wilbur, President Taft seemed completely at ease among all the reporters, stopping to joke with them. When one reporter asked him whether he would consider going up in a flying machine, the president looked down at himself and commented, "I would love to, but I do not think I have an aeronautical figure." He was six feet two inches tall and weighed three hundred pounds. Everyone laughed, and the following morning the newspapers featured cartoons showing a corpulent President Taft weighing down a flying machine.

Although Orville and Wilbur took every precaution to avoid private interviews with reporters, they did relent and allow Kate Carew, one of the first women journalists and a reporter for the New York World, to ask them a few questions in the lobby of their hotel.

Kate got right to the point and began peppering the brothers with questions. Orville quickly noticed that she seemed more interested in what he and Wilbur thought about flying than in the mechanics of flying machines, which both of them would have preferred to talk about.

"Will flying machines ever be transporting large numbers of people as railroads do?" Kate asked.

"No," Wilbur said. "That would be too expensive."

"What about carrying freight?"

"Nope," Wilbur again replied, matter-of-factly.

Then Orville chimed in. "They could be used for first-class mail."

"That's about all in time of peace," Wilbur added.

"And in war?" Kate asked.

"Chiefly for scouting, reconnoitering the enemy's position, and so on," Wilbur replied.

"But not for transporting troops?"

"No," Orville answered. "You'd need too many of them."

"And what about dropping bombs and things on people?"

"Oh, yes, you never can tell," Wilbur said.

"To come back to the realm of sport then, they'll be the automobiles of the air?" Kate asked.

"Yes, with no tires to burst," Wilbur said dryly.

"And when every respectable family on Fifth Avenue and the upper West Side has one or two Flyers, and the air is full of them in pleasant weather, what will be the possibility of a summer trip to San Francisco?" Kate asked, looking at Orville.

Orville paused for a moment before answering. "That'll be practicable enough," he began. "By that time there are sure to be stations in every town for the landing and launching of flying machines and the supply of gasoline. So you could make the San Francisco trip in stages of say five hundred miles, flying, say, ten hours a day. The figures are only approximate, but they're well within present possibilities.

That would make it an easy six-day trip, and, of course, you could shorten the time by flying twelve, fourteen, or more hours each day."

"And what is the best you can do with the Flyer for the plain businessman after an exhausting day downtown?" Kate then asked.

Wilbur looked at Orville, as if signaling him to answer this question as well. Orville felt embarrassed. He did not quite know how to answer it. Then a thought struck him. "If he didn't want to make a trip to any particular place," Orville began, "the businessman could fly up to a great height, shut off the motor, and soar about on ascending currents of air as the great birds do."

"And which of you two was the first to think of flying?" Kate asked, changing her line of questioning.

"I don't know," Wilbur replied.

"I guess we both thought of it together, didn't we?" Orville said.

"It kind of developed," Wilbur added.

"You said one day that you'd like to fly, and it kind of started from there," Orville added, looking at Wilbur.

Both Orville and Wilbur were glad when the interview with Kate Carew was over. Neither of them liked to answer questions like that, and Miss Carew sure had plenty of questions to ask.

Following the presentation at the White House, Orville and Wilbur returned to Dayton, where the city held an official welcome home for its two native sons. All the businesses in town were closed for two days of parades, ceremonies, and banquets. Orville was glad that his father had lived to see the event, especially since all five of the Wright children and seven grandchildren were there and sat on the stage together.

After the celebration in Dayton, it was off to Fort Myer, with a rebuilt Flyer to finish the tests that had been interrupted by Orville's crash. During the remaining flight tests, the Flyer was clocked at forty-two miles per hour in the air, enough speed to earn the army contract with two miles to spare. Winning the contract, much more than the parades and medals, represented success to Wilbur and Orville. The brothers had conquered the air, and now their own government had decided to invest in their flying machines. Indeed, the Wright brothers had been very successful since taking to the air. They had managed to amass over a quarter of a million dollars in contracts, prizes, and fees, with the promise of many times more that amount to come in the future.

Upon successful completion of the tests at Fort Myer, Orville and Wilbur decided to separate a third time to undertake various flying assignments. Wilbur would stay in the United States to fly at the huge celebration New York City was planning. The celebration was to commemorate Henry Hudson's navigation of the Hudson River in 1609 and the starting in 1807 of Robert Fulton's steamboat service on the river between Albany and New York. Six countries were taking part in the event, which would provide a unique opportunity for the Wright brothers to showcase their Flyer. The city had agreed to pay Wilbur $15,000 if he would fly from Governor's

Island up the Hudson to Grant's Tomb and back, a distance of twenty miles. While Wilbur was doing this, Orville would head to Germany to convince the Kaiser to buy the Wright Flyer.

Katharine went along with Orville to Germany, and the two of them were lodged in one of Berlin's best hotels and given a German interpreter for the length of their stay. Everything went well on the trip. During one of his demonstration flights, Orville managed to stay in the air for over an hour and ascended to a new record altitude of sixteen hundred feet. And Crown Prince Friedrich Wilhelm insisted on flying with Orville on one of the flights, becoming the first member of a royal family to take to the air.

While Orville was in Germany, news reached him that Wilbur was the darling of the New York City celebrations. Wilbur not only had completed the twenty-mile course in the Flyer but also, on a second flight, had swooped around the Statue of Liberty in an amazing show of aeronautical control. The crowd of one million who witnessed the event loved it. And the newspapers went wild. *Harper's Weekly* devoted the entire front page of the October 9, 1909, issue to a photograph of Wilbur and the Flyer circling the Statue of Liberty's skirts, with a headline that read, "A New Thing Came Today."

When Orville returned to the United States, he and Wilbur agreed that it was time to get serious about mass-producing Wright Flyers in a commercial factory. Investors clamored to be a part of the new venture, and in November 1909 the new Wright

Company was formally incorporated. Work on a new factory in Dayton began right away.

Now, more than ever, it was important for the people of America to see and understand the potential of flying machines. This led Orville and Wilbur to one inescapable fact: they would have to train more pilots in order to exhibit their Flyers from Washington, D.C., to San Francisco.

The brothers also set to work designing the Model B Flyer. This was a two-seater craft with a forty-horsepower engine and a horizontal elevator that they placed at the back of the plane with the vertical rudders to form a tail. The more powerful engine meant that the catapult takeoff system was no longer needed, as the Model B could get itself into the air under its own power. A second single-seat Flyer named the Model R was also planned. The R stood for racer, and Orville and Wilbur hoped that the model would ace the competition in the many international air races that were popping up.

One particularly unpleasant distraction, however, often kept Orville and Wilbur from the task at hand. This distraction involved the legal patents they had received for their wing-warping mechanism. Their lawyer had written the patent in such a way that it covered not only the twisting of the wings but also any other way in which a wing shape could be altered in the air to increase or decrease air pressure on it. This meant, in practical terms, that virtually any method developed to control the motion of an aircraft in the air using the wings belonged to the Wright brothers.

Glenn Curtiss, one of the members of Alexander Graham Bell's Aerial Experiment Association, had developed a system using ailerons—small movable "flaps" on the wings. At first Orville and Wilbur had even given Curtiss information on how to design these ailerons, as Curtiss told them that he was interested only in research. But research soon turned to the more practical matter of making money, and Curtiss began producing airplanes with ailerons on them. When they learned what he was doing, Wilbur and Orville wrote to him referring to their patent number and asking for royalties for the ailerons, but Curtiss did not respond.

The dispute quickly turned into a complicated and public lawsuit that seemed to go on and on. To advance their lawsuit against Curtiss, Orville and Wilbur decided that they needed to protect their patents from other violators as well. In a flurry of activity, their lawyers secured patents in eight European countries and then went after patent violators in those countries as well.

As the protracted legal proceedings dragged on, the task of designing and building the Model B and Model R Flyers continued. Orville also trained nine young men to become pilots. The young men were soon the folk heroes of the day. One of Orville's students, a man by the name of Calbraith Rodgers, undertook the challenge of flying coast to coast. This was in response to a prize of $50,000 put up by newspaper baron William Randolph Hearst for the first man to fly the distance in less than thirty days. Rodgers set out from New York on September

17, 1911, and made it to Long Beach, California, on December 10, 1911. It was a remarkable feat, especially since Orville and Wilbur had made their tentative first powered flights only eight years before.

Four months later Calbraith Rodgers died in a plane crash while trying to avoid a flock of seagulls. His death brought the number of aircraft fatalities to over one hundred. Among these one hundred fatalities were Charles Rolls, the cofounder of Rolls-Royce, and five of the men Orville had trained to fly. Orville and Wilbur discussed the number of pilots they had lost while giving demonstration flights and decided that it was time for them to get out of the exhibition flying business. Instead they would concentrate solely on building Flyers and defending their patents, along with one domestic matter—building a mansion for themselves on a seventeen-acre lot in Oakwood, located two miles southeast of downtown Dayton. The brothers had named the new estate Hawthorn Hill, and Orville was busy tweaking the plans for the new house so that building could begin.

At the end of April Wilbur returned from a trip to New York and Boston, and on May 2, 1912, he and Orville, accompanied by Katharine and their father, visited the Hawthorn Hill estate. As they walked over the land, Orville pointed out where the new house would sit. Wilbur once again quizzed his younger brother. "My bedroom has its own bathroom now, doesn't it, Orv?"

Orville nodded. How could he have ever forgotten? Wilbur had told him over and over again. He even wrote home once from Europe to reiterate, "I am going to have a bathroom of my own, so please make me one."

On Saturday afternoon Wilbur, after spending his morning in the upstairs office at the bicycle shop, was feeling a little under the weather. Katharine put him to bed and called for the doctor, who announced that Wilbur had a touch of malaria and should be feeling better in a few days.

When Orville heard of his brother's condition, he was not too worried. After all, the doctor had said he would be up and about in a few days. The new Model C Flyer ordered by the army was almost ready for delivery, and Orville busied himself making preparations for its delivery to Washington, D.C.

After four days, however, Wilbur was feeling no better, and the doctor visited him once more. After again examining Wilbur, he changed his diagnosis. Wilbur did not have a touch of malaria, after all. Instead he had contracted typhoid fever. Now Orville was much more concerned about his brother's condition. He recalled his own struggle with typhoid fever sixteen years before and how the disease had nearly taken his life. He hoped desperately that this would not happen to Wilbur.

But as the days rolled on, Wilbur's condition grew worse. His fever continued to climb, and it was hard for him to eat. Reuchlin returned to Dayton from Kansas, and he, Lorin, Orville, Katharine, and their father took turns sitting at Wilbur's bedside.

Orville became particularly concerned when Wilbur sent for Ezra Kuhns, a Dayton lawyer, to prepare his will. Orville was also faced with a problem. The time had come to deliver the new Model C Flyer to Washington, but Orville was reluctant to leave his brother's side. However, after talking with the doctor, he was reassured that Wilbur's condition was stable for the moment, and it would be fine for him to travel to Washington. Orville set out for Washington, D.C., on Thursday, May 16.

Orville made the delivery of the Model C Flyer in Washington and caught the first train back to Dayton. By the evening of Monday, May 20, he was back at Wilbur's bedside. Over the next few days, Wilbur seemed a little better each day. Orville's hopes began to rise. Perhaps Wilbur was going to make a full recovery from the typhoid just as Orville had done years before.

But on May 26, the spirits of everyone in the Wright household began to flag. Wilbur's condition began to deteriorate rapidly. Two days later the doctor announced that there was now no hope for Wilbur's making a full recovery. Orville could scarcely believe it. He felt numb.

In the early hours of the morning on Wednesday, May 30, 1912, Wilbur Wright died at the age of forty-five. When Orville learned of his brother's death, he felt very alone inside. He and Wilbur had not only been brothers but also best friends, confidants, and collaborators in solving the problem of flight. Now Wilbur was gone.

When news of Wilbur's death was made public, telegrams of condolence and flowers began flooding into the Wright house on Hawthorn Street. On

June 1 Wilbur's casket was moved to the First Presbyterian Church of Dayton for public viewing. Twenty-five thousand people filed past his body to pay their last respects and say good-bye. A half-hour funeral service was held at the church, and then Wilbur's body was taken to Woodland Cemetery to be buried in the family plot.

At three thirty in the afternoon, as Wilbur's casket was being carried from the First Presbyterian Church, all of the businesses and industries in Dayton came to a halt for three minutes of silence in honor of Wilbur.

Only members of the Wright family were present at the graveside as Wilbur was buried. As Orville watched his brother's coffin slowly being lowered into the grave, tears welled in his eyes. Orville wondered how he was ever going to go on without his brother around. But then his mind went back to his mother's funeral twenty-three years before. He had felt sad and lonely then and had wondered how he could go on without her encouragement and the confidence she had in him. But somehow he had gone on, and now he had to find the courage to go on like that again.

Chapter 16

Life Goes On for Orville

Less than a year after Wilbur's death, disaster struck Dayton. It was Easter Sunday, March 23, 1913, when the rain began to fall. Orville was surprised at how heavy it was, and it did not look as though it was going to let up anytime soon. In fact, it was raining even heavier the next day, and the Miami River was beginning to rise. Much of Dayton was low-lying and sat at the confluence of the Miami, Stillwater, and Mad rivers with Wolf Creek, so when one of the rivers began to rise, the residents of the city got a little nervous. Orville, though, was kept too busy taking care of various business matters to notice. The rain was just an inconvenience to him.

On the morning of Tuesday, March 25, it was still raining heavily as Orville and Katharine left the

house on Hawthorn Street to attend an appointment on the other side of town, leaving their father
home alone. As they made their way across town,
they were unaware that because of the heavy rain,
the earthen dam holding back Loramie Reservoir in
Shelby County well to the north of Dayton had col-
lapsed and a wall of water was headed down the
Miami River Valley. While Orville and Katharine were
at their appointment, the wall of water reached
Dayton, bursting the levee and flooding into the low-
lying areas, particularly West Dayton.

When Orville and Katharine tried to get back
home after their appointment, the water had risen to
such a dangerous level that they were forced to take
shelter in a friend's house located on high ground.
When they learned that the floodwater was eight feet
deep on Hawthorn Street, Orville and Katharine
became very concerned about their father.

Orville spent a sleepless night at the house on
Summit Street, worrying about something in addition to his father. All of the photographic negatives of
the flight experiments at Kitty Hawk and Huffman's
Prairie between 1900 and 1905 were stored in the
shed at the back of the Wright house. The shed was
undoubtedly underwater by now. And the water in
the vicinity of West Third Street, where the bicycle
shop was located, was reported to be twelve feet
deep. Orville reckoned that that depth of water could
well flood the upstairs office where all of the records
of the invention of the airplane were stored.

In the morning Orville and Katharine received
some good news. A passerby reported that he had

seen their father being carried away in a canoe sent to rescue their neighbor, Mrs. Wagner, and their father was safe at a house on Williams Street. But the day also brought bad news for Orville. Despite the rain and floodwater, gas from ruptured gas lines had caught fire, and many of the buildings on and near West Third Street were on fire. As he looked out across the city, Orville could see the glow of the flames, but he could do nothing about the situation.

By March 30 the rain had stopped and the floodwater had receded far enough for Orville and Katharine to make their way back to West Dayton. The house on Hawthorn Street was a soggy mess. Everything downstairs was ruined. Orville quickly made his way to the shed at the back of the house to see how the photographic negatives had fared. He expected the worst, but as he located the negatives, he was amazed at what good condition they were in for having spent so much time underwater. The emulsion on a few of the glass plate negatives was beginning to peel, but none of the negatives was a total loss. And the most important negative—the shot John Daniels had snapped of Orville on the 1903 Flyer moments after takeoff on its first flight— had one small piece of emulsion peeling at one corner, leaving the rest of the image intact and in good condition.

After discovering that the negatives were safe, Orville made his way to the bicycle shop on West Third Street. He wasn't even sure that the shop would still be standing. To his delight it was. Many of the buildings in the area around it had been burned, but the fire had not touched the bicycle shop. Like the house on Hawthorn Street, everything downstairs was ruined. Fortunately, although the twelve feet of water had reached to the downstairs ceiling, it had not seeped into the office above. All of the important papers regarding the development of the airplane were safe. And still in its packing crate in a shed at the back of the bicycle shop, the original 1903 Flyer was mud-covered but unscathed.

And there was more good news for Orville. The Wright Company aircraft factory was located on high ground and had not been flooded. Neither had the Hawthorn Hill estate, where construction of the new house was well under way. Orville considered himself very lucky, especially since the flood had killed 371 people and done $100 million of damage to Dayton.

The following year, 1914, began on a much more promising note. After five years of wrangling, the U.S. Circuit Court of Appeals in New York ruled in favor of the Wright Company in its patent lawsuit against Glenn Curtiss. However, it was not long before Curtiss appealed the court's decision, and a whole new round of suing began. But by this time something even more annoying was in the works.

The 1914 annual report from the Smithsonian Institution stated that Samuel Pierpont Langley's Great Aerodrome was "the first aeroplane capable of sustained free flight with a man." The statement was based on a strange set of circumstances that had to do with the struggle over patents. Albert Zahm, an acquaintance of Orville's, was named the head of the new aeronautical office of the Smithsonian Institution. Zahm was a friend of Curtiss's and had testified in court on Curtiss's behalf against the Wright brothers. After he was appointed to his new position, Zahm got together with Curtiss and the two of them decided to rebuild Langley's Great Aerodrome to see whether it could have flown if it had not plummeted into the Potomac River upon launch. If it was proved that it could have flown, Zahm and Curtiss could argue that Wilbur and Orville had not invented powered flight, after all, thereby weakening their legal case. The Smithsonian Institution went along with the idea, enamored with the thought that their former secretary might be awarded such an honor.

The tests of the Great Aerodrome were not conducted fairly, however. In restoring the Great Aerodrome, Curtiss secretly modified the craft using the latest technology. He changed the shape of the rudder, added more stays to the wings, increased the horsepower of the engine, and fitted the craft with pontoons for landing. With all of these changes, the men were able to get the Great Aerodrome airborne on June 2, 1914, at Lake Keuka near Hammondsport, New York, where it flew for three thousand feet. With this result, Zahm pronounced Samuel Pierpont Langley to be "The First In Powered Flight." Following the flight, Curtiss restored the Great Aerodrome back to its original 1903 specifications, after which the craft went on display at the Smithsonian

Institution. Anyone looking at the Aerodrome and reading the plaque beneath it would conclude that this exact aeroplane had flown for three thousand feet. Orville was furious at this outcome, but he had other things on his mind, and he decided to wait and see what would happen next.

In the spring of 1914, Orville, Katharine, and Bishop Wright moved into the new house at the Hawthorn Hill estate in Dayton. The many visitors who walked up the long, winding driveway to the place said it reminded them of the White House, and Orville had to agree. The insides of the house were even more impressive than the neoclassical-columned exterior. Orville had planned every detail of the house, including the vacuum-cleaning system set inside the walls, water pipes that ran through the back of the ice chest and delivered ice-cold water from the kitchen faucet, and a toaster that clamped the bread between two hot iron plates, producing the perfect slice of compressed, browned toast. These simple things brought Orville immense pleasure, while dealing with the ongoing court battle and managing corporations did not.

Still embroiled in court proceedings over the patent lawsuit, and without Wilbur at his side, Orville lost interest in running the Wright Company. He hated attending board meetings and coping with the masses of paperwork he was expected to wade through. So in October 1915 he sold the company to a group of Manhattan investors for $1.5 million. As part of the deal, he agreed to stay on with the company as the chief consulting engineer for one year.

The sale of the company provided Orville with plenty of money to live comfortably and to help support his family for the rest of his life. In addition, he was free to pursue whatever he liked.

By 1915 Europe was fully embroiled in World War I. As a result of the war, interest in airplanes reached a fevered pitch. Airplanes were being used to spot the enemy on the ground and spy on what they were up to, and they also were being experimented with as a means of dropping bombs on the enemy.

In 1916 the Wright Company merged with the Glenn L. Martin Company to become the Wright-Martin Aircraft Corporation. Orville was retained as the chief consulting engineer at the new company. A year later he established the Wright Aeronautical Laboratory in Dayton.

On the morning of April 3, 1917, Bishop Wright did not come down for breakfast. This was unusual, and Orville went upstairs to wake him. He found his father dead in bed. Milton Wright was eighty-nine years old, and he was buried in the family plot in Woodland Cemetery beside his wife, Susan, and his son Wilbur. It seemed hard for Orville to believe that Wilbur had been dead for five years now. Sometimes he still found himself thinking that Wilbur was in the next room and would burst through the door at any moment with some scientific question to discuss.

Four days after Milton Wright's funeral, the United States entered World War I. By now four wealthy men from Dayton had asked Orville to become a consulting engineer for their company, which they called the Dayton-Wright Company. Orville agreed, and the company immediately won a contract with the United States government to supply 4,400 aircraft, 4,000 warplanes, and 400 trainers. The Dayton-Wright Company had produced only a fraction of this number of airplanes when the war came to an end in 1918. But the ongoing work of manufacturing them kept Orville very busy.

In January 1920 President Woodrow Wilson appointed Orville to be a member of the National Advisory Committee for Aeronautics, or NACA, as it was soon shortened to. NACA was President Wilson's brainchild. The committee's sole purpose was to conduct research and development to help the United States aircraft industry. The position suited Orville fine. Once a year he got to meet with some of the best minds in America, not to plan business strategy but to talk about the science of flight.

Soon after attending the first meeting of NACA in Virginia, another death struck the Wright family. This time it was 59-year-old Reuchlin.

Another unpleasant event followed quickly. A public feud erupted between Orville and the Smithsonian Institution over the Langley Aerodrome affair and over who was the true "father of flight." The feud boiled to the surface after Englishman Griffith Brewer visited Orville. Orville had met Griffith on his first visit to England, and the two had become good friends. During this current visit with Orville, Griffith told how he had visited Hammondsport, New York, during 1914 to see the test flight of the Great Aerodrome. Not only that, he had toured the facility where the modifications had been made to the craft and was able to identify what those changes were. He even had photographs to prove it.

Armed with this information, Orville felt that the time was right to challenge the Smithsonian Institution head-on. He was particularly incensed by the plaque that accompanied the display of the Great Aerodrome, describing it as "the first man-carrying aeroplane in the history of the world capable of sustained free flight. Invented, built, and tested over the Potomac River by Samuel Pierpont Langley in 1903. Successfully flown at Hammondsport, N.Y., June 2, 1914."

For two months Orville and Griffith worked together on compiling a detailed list of improvements that had been made to fly the Great Aerodrome. Griffith then published the detailed list under his own name in a paper titled *Aviation's Greatest Controversy*. Despite publication of the paper, no one at the Smithsonian Institution was prepared to back down on its claims regarding Langley and the Great Aerodrome. Frustrated, Orville decided on another course of action. He was in the process of restoring the 1903 Flyer for an exhibit at the Massachusetts Institute of Technology. He did not know what he was going to do with the craft when the exhibit was over, but now he had a plan. The 1903 Flyer would go to the Science Museum in London, England, on loan until the Smithsonian Institution gave him a public apology.

With this decided, Orville hoped that he could live a quiet and orderly life. He was now fifty years old, and he did not predict any more life-altering changes. He had plenty of money to buffer him from almost anything, or so he thought. But five years later, in 1926, Katharine made an extraordinary announcement. Henry Haskell, an old college friend recently widowed, had asked her to marry him, and she had accepted. There was going to be a wedding, and fifty-two-year-old Katharine Wright was to be the bride!

Orville was stunned. He had no idea that Katharine and Henry were in love. But quickly his shock turned to anger. He had assumed that his sister would live on at Hawthorn Hill with him for the rest of his life, but now she was planning to move to Kansas. He stopped talking to her and did not even wish her well when she packed her bags and left the house. The rift became very deep. Orville could not forgive Katharine for abandoning him to a house filled with memories but no relatives. Other members of the Wright family tried to reconcile the two of them, but Orville would have none of it. He soldiered on alone.

On December 17, 1928, Orville was back on the Outer Banks of North Carolina. It was the twenty-fifth anniversary of his first powered flight in 1903, and the government had decided to mark Orville and Wilbur's achievement by erecting a permanent memorial atop the sand dunes at Kill Devil Hills.

The group of official guests gathered at the top of the dunes as the national anthem was played, but the blustery wind made it almost impossible to hear the speeches that followed. Orville smiled to himself. It was the wind that had drawn him and

Wilbur to these dunes in the first place. At the end of the ceremony, a cornerstone was laid for the obelisk memorial that would be erected on the site in the years to come.

Following the ceremony the gathered crowd made its way down the side of the dunes to a place where a granite boulder had been set in the sand. The boulder marked the exact spot where Orville had lifted off to make the first manned, powered flight in the Flyer in 1903. Orville stood beside Amelia Earhart during this ceremony. Once again the national anthem was played, and speeches were made, but Orville didn't hear much of it. His mind had rolled back to that day twenty-five years before when he and Wilbur had made history together. What a day it had been. (Orville would make one last trip to Kill Devil Hills, in 1932, for the official dedication of the finished memorial.)

Two months after the cornerstone-laying ceremony at Kill Devil Hills, Secretary of War Dwight Davis presented Orville and Wilbur (posthumously) with the Distinguished Flying Cross. Orville was touched by this honor, but within a week it was all but forgotten. News came from Kansas City that Katharine was seriously ill with pneumonia. At first Orville did not want to visit her, but his brother Lorin urged him to forgive his sister and go to her side. Orville arrived in Kansas City just in time to see Katharine draw her last breath. It was with very mixed emotions that he arranged for Katharine's burial beside his parents and Wilbur at Woodland Cemetery in Dayton.

In 1931, Orville Wright celebrated his sixtieth birthday surrounded by his nephews, nieces, friends, and neighbors and wondered what life might still hold for him.

Chapter 17

"A Man Who Was Just One of Folks Like Us"

The date was April 16, 1938, what would have been Wilbur's seventy-first birthday. Orville wandered around their Hawthorn Street home, past the bedroom he and Wilbur had shared as boys, downstairs and through the kitchen and out onto the veranda. He stood holding the railing he had turned on a lathe more years ago now than he cared to remember. The crowd cheered and waved at him as he stepped outside. Orville looked down the street toward a Cape Cod windmill and then in the other direction toward Thomas Edison's laboratory. How amazing it was to see his old house in such a new setting. Ford had purchased the place from the Wrights' old laundrywoman in Dayton, disassembled it, and brought it to Dearborn, Michigan, where he had it rebuilt. Ford had also purchased the building on West Third Street that housed the Wright Cycle Company. And now it too sat among the other famous and important buildings that Ford had relocated from around the United States to what he called Greenfield Village, in Dearborn.

It was a strange day for Orville as he realized that the most mundane things of his and Wilbur's lives were now being viewed as national treasures.

A year later war broke out in Europe, and closer to home, Orville's brother Lorin died. This left Orville as the only surviving sibling of the Wright clan. Loneliness engulfed Orville as he thought about all the people who were now gone. He felt like a living relic himself at times.

The accolades continued to be heaped on Orville for his achievements in flight. He received a total of eleven honorary degrees, including degrees from Yale, Harvard, the University of Michigan, and the University of Munich. A number of these degrees conferred on him the title "Dr. Wright." This greatly amused Orville, since he had not even finished high school.

On August 19, 1940, Orville attended the official dedication of the Wilbur and Orville Wright Memorial in Dayton, located near Huffman's Prairie. Of all the memorials commemorating the places where the Wright brothers had flown, Huffman's Prairie was the one that had been the least touched by the passage of time. As Orville strolled over its pocked surface, he could see the 1904 Flyer laboring to take off, with Wilbur at the controls and Charles Taylor holding a stopwatch to time the flight.

Whenever he saw one of the large, new, four-engine commercial aircraft that were now being built and flown, Orville never ceased to marvel at the revolution that he and Wilbur had started. Who would have guessed that such big airplanes, with such a broad array of uses, were to flow from those small beginnings at Kitty Hawk, North Carolina.

Life continued on, though Orville suffered from constant back pain as arthritis set into his old injuries. Still, he was glad to live to see the Smithsonian Institution finally apologize for misrepresenting the Great Aerodrome as being the first powered machine capable of manned flight. It was enormously satisfying for him to hold in his hand the brochure titled *The 1914 Tests of the Langley "Aerodrome,"* which apologized for and retracted the Smithsonian's former statements regarding Langley and the Great Aerodrome.

With the Smithsonian-Wright controversy finally over, Orville agreed to have the 1903 Flyer returned from England to be displayed at the Smithsonian. However, with World War II raging in Europe, it was unsafe to bring the Flyer back across the Atlantic Ocean, and so Orville wrote a letter of intent to do so as soon as the war was over.

When the war ended in 1945, Wilbur set to work restoring the 1905 Flyer. This was to be the last major project of his life. On October 10, 1947, as he was running up some steps, Orville suffered a heart attack. He was taken to the hospital and placed in an oxygen tent. As his health improved, Orville, being Orville, became interested in how to make the oxygen tent more efficient.

When he was released from the hospital, Orville was told to slow down. But his brain was too active to let him sit still reading a book for long. He was soon up and about, but two months later, on January 30, 1948, Orville suffered a second heart attack. This one he did not survive. He died at the age of seventy-six.

News of Orville's death spread quickly around the world, and dignitaries from many countries showed up in Dayton to attend his funeral. The funeral was much more elaborate than Orville would have wanted it to be, but he had accepted a long time ago that his fame came at a price and that a part of him belonged to the American people.

Schoolchildren were released from classes on the day of the funeral, flags were flown at half-staff across the country, and thousands of people lined the streets of Dayton to pay homage to their hometown hero. The minister conducting the funeral service praised Orville as "a man who was just one of folks like us—middle class, mid-Western American, with simple, devout parents, and a simple and modest way of life."

Orville was laid to rest next to Wilbur. The brothers were together again. As Orville's body was lowered into the ground, four jet fighters circled overhead in formation and dipped their wings. Orville Wright would have loved the sight.

On November 22, 1948, the 1903 Flyer arrived back in the United States from London and was delivered to the Smithsonian Institution. The Flyer was formally presented to the Smithsonian in a ceremony on December 17, forty-five years to the minute after Orville had first lifted off the beach in it at Kill Devil Hills in 1903. The Flyer was hung in the North Hall of the Institution, along with some of the most treasured pieces in American history, including George Washington's uniform, Thomas Jefferson's writing desk, and Benjamin Franklin's stove. Finally the Flyer was where it had always belonged. The words on the exhibit read:

THE ORIGINAL WRIGHT BROTHERS AEROPLANE
THE WORLD'S FIRST POWER-DRIVEN,
HEAVIER-THAN-AIR MACHINE IN WHICH MAN
MADE FREE, CONTROLLED, AND SUSTAINED FLIGHT
INVENTED AND BUILT BY WILBUR AND ORVILLE WRIGHT
FLOWN BY THEM AT KITTY HAWK, NORTH CAROLINA
DECEMBER 17, 1903
BY ORIGINAL SCIENTIFIC RESEARCH THE WRIGHT BROTHERS
DISCOVERED THE PRINCIPLES OF HUMAN FLIGHT
AS INVENTORS, BUILDERS, AND FLYERS THEY
FURTHER DEVELOPED THE AEROPLANE,
TAUGHT MAN TO FLY, AND OPENED
THE ERA OF AVIATION

Bibliography

Collins, Mary. *Airborne: A Photobiography of Wilbur and Orville Wright.* National Geographic, 2003.

Crouch, Tom. *The Bishop's Boys: A Life of Wilbur and Orville Wright.* W. W. Norton, 1989.

Culick, Fred E. C., and Spencer Dunmore. *On Great White Wings: The Wright Brothers and the Race for Flight.* Hyperion, 2001.

Heppenheimer, T. A. *First Flight: The Wright Brothers and the Invention of the Airplane.* John Wiley & Sons, 2003.

Howard, Fred. *Wilbur and Orville: A Biography of the Wright Brothers.* Alfred A. Knopf, 1987.

Tobin, James. *To Conquer the Air: The Wright Brothers and the Great Race for Flight.* Free Press, 2003.

Walsh, John Evangelist. *One Day at Kitty Hawk: The Untold Story of the Wright Brothers and the Airplane.* Thomas Y. Crowell Company, 1975.

Wolko, Howard S. (Editor). *The Wright Flyer: An Engineering Perspective.* Smithsonian Institution Press, 1987.

Janet and Geoff Benge are a husband and wife writing team with more than twenty years of writing experience. Janet is a former elementary school teacher. Geoff holds a degree in history. Together they have a passion to make history come alive for a new generation of readers.

Originally from New Zealand, the Benges make their home in the Orlando, Florida, area.

Also from Janet and Geoff Benge...

More adventure-filled biographies for ages 10 to 100!